# IKIGAI

**The Japanese Secret To Discovering Your Life Purpose And Living Days Full Of Meaning, Happiness And Love.**

**By**

**Sally Cress**

**Legal & Disclaimer**

The information contained in this book and its contents is not designed to replace or take the place of any form of medical or professional advice; and is not meant to replace the need for independent medical, financial, legal or other professional advice or services, as may be required. The content and information in this book have been provided for educational and entertainment purposes only.

The content and information contained in this book has been compiled from sources deemed reliable, and it is accurate to the best of the Author's knowledge, information and belief. However, the Author cannot guarantee its accuracy and validity and cannot be held liable for any errors and/or omissions. Further, changes are periodically made to this book as and when needed. Where appropriate and/or necessary, you must consult a professional (including but not limited to your doctor, attorney, financial advisor or such other professional advisor) before using any of the suggested remedies, techniques, or information in this book.

Upon using the contents and information contained in this book, you agree to hold harmless the Author from and against any damages, costs, and expenses, including any legal fees potentially resulting from the application of any of the information provided by this book. This disclaimer applies to any loss, damages or injury caused by the use and application, whether directly or indirectly, of any advice or information presented, whether for breach of contract, tort, negligence, personal injury, criminal intent, or under any other cause of action.

**You agree to accept all risks of using the information presented inside this book.**

You agree that by continuing to read this book, where appropriate and/or necessary, you shall consult a professional (including but not limited to your doctor, attorney, or financial advisor or such other advisor as needed) before using any of the suggested remedies, techniques, or information in this book.

# TABLE OF CONTENTS

# INTRODUCTION

As time passes, we all realize that life is not as simple as we thought. When we are young, we are full of desires and expectations, ready to face the world with hope and patience. However, time - and experiences - frequently shape us negatively by preventing us from seeing things as they are. And this is how each of us experiences dark times. Moments when the sun appears to be a distant memory. However, Japanese wisdom holds the key to living a peaceful and satisfying life. This is what it is.

First and foremost, locate your Ikigai.

Many of you have most likely never heard of this term before. It's a shame because you should know that everyone, without exception, needs your own Ikigai. Time is tough to translate, but it can be defined as the reason for its existence. You choose between waking up every morning and loving the person next to you. However, the main difficulty is determining which of us is our Ikigai. It is not easy to find, as many people believe. Each of us has unique characteristics that contribute to the enormous puzzle of life.

You must weigh your inner strengths and weaknesses and understand what is being asked. You possess an important (and unique) feature of the universe. It is your responsibility to discover about it and learn how to use it to benefit yourself and others. Understanding the foundation of your dreams is most likely the key

1

to your success. You will never find your Ikigai if you only do what you think is proper, necessary, or the method of "reviving." Follow your heart and start doing what you enjoy. Everything else will fall into place on its own.

Who Are You?

What do you do when you get up in the morning? Run fast why do you have to go to work? And in the afternoon? Are you still running to get home and do all the chores? Probably yes, because this is a typical life that leads us only to apparent happiness (money, a socially active life) but makes us thoroughly lose ourselves and the meaning of life. Spending time running without pausing to observe and listen to live's purpose and immense heartbeat will never lead to happiness. Perhaps he will provide us with some daily bribe from purchasing a material good, but he will never be able to penetrate our hearts. Yes, because the only way to find peace is to be self-sufficient. But every day, we ask ourselves, "Do we know who we are?" Or do we simply know who we've chosen to be?

Remember the Five Pillars of Happy Living.

Once we've discovered ourselves, all we have to do is learn to spend time with the person we've found we are (really). Do we put in the effort? Yes, perhaps. However, we must prioritize ourselves over money. So we don't have to make excuses and stick to the three fundamental pillars of happiness:

-To Find Happiness, Begin Small.

Whatever you decide, begin with small steps. We'd all like to see our lives transform overnight. However, change that occurs gradually and gradually is often the most effective, best, and longest-lasting.

-Forget about yourself to be happy.

-To forget about oneself means to take off the mask we have worn so far to please others and society. However, we must no longer be focused on ourselves. We must recognize that we are only a drop in a vast ocean and that only by being a part of the whole can we find peace.

-The keys to happiness are harmony and sustainability.

We must never forget to live in harmony with creation. We cannot believe that by destroying our surroundings, we will be able to live peacefully. If we are a part of a larger universe, everything that comes our way is a part of us: let us use it to help ourselves, and other creatures grow.

-Joy For The Little Things

Human beings tend to complain. He can only understand the importance of small things when he has lost them. But the secret to happiness is to appreciate what we already have rather than seeking what we do not yet have. You should consider yourself fortunate if you can walk, get out of bed, eat, and sleep in the heat. And if the person you love is next to you and the first person you see when you wake up every morning, you can declare happiness.

-To be happy, stay in the present moment.

The final fundamental pillar is to avoid excessive mental travel between the past and the future. Savor the flavor of the food as you eat it, and as you take the one, you love by the hand. Do not make mechanical gestures.

Enjoy every beautiful moment of your life because the past is gone and the future is unknown. Why give thought space when you can have unique sensations? Learn to observe and listen if you want to experience true happiness firsthand. Life will appear to your eyes as it truly is: a wonderful dream.

Throughout the book, we will explain how to achieve your ikigai by following these five pillars, and we will teach you techniques to add balance and serenity to your life.

Suppose it is true that the life of each of us has highs, lows, dark moments, and moments in which we want to disappear and are overwhelmed by pain and uncertainty. In that case, it is equally valid that we can improve ourselves, know our weaknesses and, despite those, or thanks to them, as some concepts of Japanese philosophy teach us, we can start again and make the best of ourselves.

# CHAPTER 1

# WHAT IS IKIGAI

You may have heard it somewhere, but if you didn't know, Japan is known for the longevity of its inhabitants.

In particular, the archipelago of Okinawa, south of the country, has become part of what is called" "ue zones" "These specific areas are populated by over 100 years old, and the death rate is much lower than in other regions of the world.

Healthy eating combined with regular physical activity is essential for these people.

However, the secret of such high longevity is also due to frequent spiritual and meditative practices and the awareness of having found their purpose in life, which makes them truly happy.

And you know, happiness is essential! We all aspire to be happy. Don't you want to be? Dan Buettner, a reporter for the famous National Geographic magazine, says that in the Okinawa area, the inhabitants of the archipelago see ikigai as" "a reason to wake up in the morning".

I'm sure you will have found yourself thinking about your dream life sometimes.

What would it be like to wake up with a smile, have breakfast in peace, and start your day doing what you love most, without feeling the weight, pressure, obligation, or duty?

If it seems like a utopia to you, know that for the Japanese, it is not. Or at least for those who have found their ikigai!

What does ikigai mean?

Ikigai (生き甲斐) is a Japanese term that has no actual translation into our language.

The word " igai "s composed of "I," which means to live, and "i" "which stands for reason.

In short, it could be said that this Japanese term indicates "e" reason for living, the reason for being" "r, more simply, the" "purpose of our life" "It is often used to indicate the loved one as well.

Finding your ikigai can take some time and deep introspection, but according to Japanese culture, we all have one, even if we are sometimes unaware of it.

But let's see the foundations of this concept.

The five fundamental pillars

Ikigai is based on five essential aspects:

1. Start small

Everything starts from small things, from small daily gestures repeated over time.

Too often, we set ourselves unattainable goals, and as a result, we feel frustrated if we fail to achieve them.

The reality is that there is no considerable magic formula to achieve the success we want in a particular area of our life.

Everything is in proceeding slowly and in small steps, taking care of the details, and starting to set small concrete and measurable goals every day.

2. Forget about yourself

According to this pillar, when we are focused and immersed in doing something we like, we forget everything around us, even ourselves.

We no longer focus our inner attention on our needs but concentrate only on the activity we carry out.

It helps us control our egos and put passion and love into everything we do without the constant thought of having recognition or reward in return.

3. Harmony and sustainability

The Japanese are constantly looking for harmony and the right balance in their every action.

Our every gesture can have positive or negative consequences. We must never forget not to be too impulsive in making some choices or making certain decisions.

We are taking the time to reflect before acting helps us make more balanced choices and find the proper harmony with others and our environment.

4. The joy of little things

It is the little things that make us feel pleasure.

It is no coincidence that we often hear that happiness is right there.

Learning to appreciate what we have is essential.

What are the little things that make you happy? For example, every time I look at a sunset, I feel grateful and rejoice to be alive and to be able to admire that wonder that I find in front of my eyes. Does the same happen to you too?

5. Stay in the here and now

Staying here and now means nothing more than living in the present without focusing too much on the past or the future. The past has already happened, and we cannot do anything to change it.

The future is uncertain.

It is not worth focusing too much on it.

You have to immerse yourself in the present.

How do I know what my purpose in life is?

Calm down, don't worry, now we get there.

In the image above, what Marc Winn first came up with and defined as the ikigai diagram.

Marc decided to combine this idea with the Venn diagram, an intersection of circles, which you will most likely have studied in school and used to show the different relationships between sets.

As we already know, ikigai is what makes us feel fully realized and alive, which gives meaning to our days and a purpose to our life.

For some, it may be a sport or a job. For others, a hobby or family.

To find out your purpose, you will need to identify these four areas:

1. What you love

2. What you are good at

3. What the world needs

4. What you can get paid for

Grab a paper and start writing—a list of all the essential things you love to do.

If it can help you, think about all those things you would do even if you didn't get paid.

What are your passions?

Once you're done, re-read everything you've written and focus primarily on those things you think you're good at.

Maybe highlight or circle.

Now that you know what you're best at think about what others might need.

What could you help them with?

Finally, ask yourself if this could lead to a job.

Would anyone be willing to pay you for it?

Once you've answered all of these questions, you've probably found your ikigai!

The last thing left for you to do now is to take action.

Don't let everything you've thought about or written down be an excellent memory.

Start throwing yourself. Get involved.

Also, remember that life is here and now, and you have no time to waste.

# CHAPTER 2
# STARTS SMALL.

---

When the feeling of apathy rises or the anxiety becomes unbearable, and you feel agitated about nothing, it is perhaps time to change something in your life.

The change can be global or concern only some aspects of existence, but it shouldn't be too scary. A little fear at the beginning of every revolution is physiological and beneficial. But fear must not become terror and block us.

Think that in life, nothing is static. Therefore, we could feel decidedly better immediately by taking our habits in hand and breaking them with a novelty or a different perspective.

Negative sensations are like blocks of energy that cannot flow freely, but some simple actions can help us feel more" entered" "and more" signed" n the balance between body and mind.

Regardless of our upbringing, level of education, and social affiliation, we all have a 168-hour week.

Why do some people manage to hit so many goals while others tend to lag with the same amount of time?

If you hear the voice "want to change my life" prevailing inside you, I see no reason you can't start doing it right now!

This desire has often been repressed with the same speed with which it arrived, not only for fear of not making it but, above all, of the resistance that each of us has to change our habits.

When people want to change, they usually foresee a drastic change that they hope to accomplish in a short time and trigger a radical change. This usually happens both in the corporate world and on a personal level. Of course, revolutionizing one's life habits can be a great source of self-esteem and growth. We know that changing is not easy.

Here are the small steps you can take to change your life for the better:

-Ask simple questions to make fears disappear

The brain loves receiving questions and pays attention to providing answers to them. He accepts them until they are so demanding that they are fearful. So if you ask yourself a question like: What job can I do to get rich? Your brain-sensing fear suppresses creativity and begins to freeze as self-defense. If, on the other hand, you ask yourself simple and calm questions, you avoid this reaction, bypassing fears and finding the right concentration to find solutions. From today try to ask simple questions like: What can I do for five minutes a day to improve my life? Remember that if you repeat the question for several days or weeks, your brain will not be able to ignore it, and at some point, it will start producing the answers.

-Learn to think small

Often, we have to face commitments that are not suited to our character or abilities. Many people think that by jumping headlong, they can overcome these obstacles. The latest findings in neurology confirm that the brain learns more quickly in tiny steps. It is also possible to practice in an imaginary way, using a sensory and total immersion, because the brain does not recognize that it is not carrying out the fictional activity.

Would you like to be able to drive in a relaxed way in traffic, without getting anxious? Imagine yourself in this situation. You are going calmly and with a clear mind while you hear the horns of other motorists. Think about being friendly to other drivers and letting them pass as they try to get out of a parking lot. Try to repeat this exercise every day. Try to imagine yourself in the worst situations until you feel ready to take action. By then, your mental sculpture should have already created new habits.

-Take small actions.

After you have practiced the simple questions and small thoughts, begin to act. By carrying out the less striking actions that may seem trivial, we can overcome all obstacles. Don't worry if the first few gestures will be negligible. Do you want to keep your home tidy? Choose an area, perhaps the bathroom, and spend only 5 minutes a day tidying it up. This low-key, non-strenuous action that takes a short time can fool the brain into believing there is no need to worry about such a small change. This way, you can create tiny daily actions that bring you new habits.

Start solving micro-problems

We all have numerous activities to do, and our day is full of commitments, so in a rush to reach a goal, we minimize the minor annoyances to avoid facing them. Of course, none of us like to make mistakes, and since minor problems can often arise severe and very important for all of us to learn to spot the minor signs as soon as they appear. We can no longer ignore the little alarm bells that could turn into big disasters or block our change process if we genuinely want to change.

-Treat yourself to the small rewards.

Small rewards are a great incentive not to procrastinate and finish a task. They can also stimulate inner motivation by being a form of recognition rather than material gain. Before establishing the rewards, remember that they must be:

-Appropriate to the goal:

Adapted to the person and free or inexpensive.

Here are my favorite rewards: a walk, a phone call to a friend, having breakfast at the bar in the morning, a new book, a self-compliment, a trip to the mountains, or a coffee in good company. To find the appropriate reward and then enjoy it.

-Recognize the crucial details.

When you want to initiate a change and are scared, stuck or anxious, look for the little hidden details. Of course, it's not always easy because it takes a truly open mind to find the potential in the tiny details. This way, you will find many opportunities for creative breakthroughs and daily improvements.

This is an efficient philosophy that can help you improve your life. It also does not force you to take an inflexible and rigid attitude that, in the long run, could lead you to abandon your intentions. You change in a gentle way respecting your times and your personality. It is a process that encourages me to continually improve myself and constantly set new goals to be achieved obviously in small steps.

# CHAPTER 3

# THE KAIZEN

---

The term KAIZEN derives from the Japanese and is composed of two words:

KAI, which means change, improvement.

ZEN indicates the concept of good, better.

Masaaki Imai coined the term at the end of the eighties of the twentieth century to indicate the business model linked to the Japanese industry, particularly Toyota.

In everyday language, we usually speak of continuous improvement. The creator of the principles behind the Kaizen method is Mr. William Edward Deming: engineer, essayist, lecturer, and business consultant.

Wanting to give a historical framework, Deming devised the method to improve the production of war factories in the United States during the Second World War, perfecting it after the war during his stay in Japan.

Let's see some history regarding what has just been said.

Kaizen method was born during the Second World War in the USA within the Training within Industry (WTI), a program created by the US Department of War to offer to consult and training services conducted on an industrial level in the war field.

Spokespersons of the Kaizen philosophy, including Mr. Deming, was a prominent figure. Instead of encouraging significant structural changes to achieve the intended results, they argued that it was preferable to introduce minor improvements, which could be implemented quickly and painlessly, even within the same day.

The main reason behind this was that there was neither the time nor the resources necessary for significant innovation in military equipment during the Second World War. It was therefore preferred to work on improving existing technologies.

Subsequently, as part of the Marshall Plan after World War II, the American occupation forces brought in experts to rebuild the Japanese industry; thanks to their contribution, the philosophy of continuous improvement was born and spread in Japan.

Dr. Deming, the spokesman for this philosophy, was awarded in 1960 by the emperor of Japan himself for having conceived, introduced, and implemented the Kaizen method in the nation, an honor called Order of the Sacred Treasure. Kaizen continuous improvement.

Since then, the Japanese Union of Scientists and Engineers (JUSE) established an annual award dedicated to those who distinguished themselves for process improvements and product quality in the name of Deming himself.

Summing up, the Kaizen method was first practiced in post-World War II Japan, influenced partly by American business models and to a greater extent by the Japanese car model from Toyota.

The term Kaizen came to light only in 1985 by the Masaaki above Imai in his first book entitled: "izen: Japanese spirit of improvement."Mr. Imai also proposed the evolution of Kaizen in his 1997 book: " MBA Kaizen: a commonsense, low-cost approach to management."

Gemba means, in simple words, the place where the product is made, for example, the assembly line of a factory.

Nowadays, companies worldwide are using the Kaizen method to improve productivity, speed, quality, and work profit while minimizing the costs, time, and effort required for the desired results.

Now that I have shown you the origins of the method let's see what continuous improvement consists of.

Kaizen method: the main concepts of continuous improvement

In this paragraph, I will show you more closely what the cornerstones of the Kaizen method are. You will understand why continuous improvement has been successful and is still widely used today.

I will start from the concept up to the concrete application of the method.

Continuous improvement in small steps

I already told you that Kaizen means continuous improvement. Some are used to give a more precise definition: continuous improvement in small steps or slow progress.

This concept is of fundamental importance to fully understand the Kaizen method. Making significant changes, be it a company or yourself, generally involves a lot of time, energy, and money. It also increases the risk of failure.

Instead, you can make a difference through little progress, even at an invisible level. When Dr. Deming was commissioned to restore Japan's devastated economy, he did not go to the heads of the companies asking for a solution plan.

Instead, he addressed his questions to the humble worker, asking every day how he could improve the situation of a small detail of his work. The sum of these small details that made the difference, the continuous incremental accumulation of small solutions, contributed to the rebirth of the Japanese economy.

The Kaizen method is based on the so-called Deming cycle or PDCA cycle. Let's see what it is. The acronym PDCA stands for:

Plan: the planning phase consists of verifying the current situation of a given process and understanding how this can be improved. We start by establishing what results from we want to obtain, and obviously, we try to apply some slight changes;

Do: in this phase, what was planned in the previous step is applied. Minor changes are used, and their effectiveness is verified through the collection of data;

Check: the collected data are then analyzed and compared to the expected results to see if the improvements obtained are in line with what was planned. An example of a test that can be conducted is the Gap Analysis;

Act: If it has been verified that what has been implemented turns out to be an improvement over the previous standards in the check phase, then this becomes the new standard for subsequent production. If this is not the case, it is necessary to study the situation better to propose other possible improvements in the future.

If a solution is proposed during the ineffective planning, the PDCA cycle can be repeated by suggesting a correction of the previous one. The cycle is repeated until the answer to the problem is found.

**Kaizen method**

Kaizen method finds a concrete application in the following aspects of the work:

-Elimination of waste: through the systematic search for better solutions, all possible sources of waste within each process are reduced;

-Standardization: one of the ways to make processes more efficient is standardization. This involves various areas of work: from procedures to equipment to the time required to perform a particular activity;

-Simplification:Very often, the easiest way to improve is to simplify. Through simplification, a lower level of staff training is required, and the possibility of error is also reduced;

Involvement of workers: the Kaizen method leverages the participation of workers. For example, cash prizes can be introduced for those who propose ideas that prove to be the most effective. Many multinationals today have this method of approach to work.

Kaizen's philosophy is applied to personal improvement.

What I have told you about the Kaizen method refers to the genesis of this philosophy, that is, to the purpose for which it was conceived starting from the Second World War: to make any process more efficient through continuous improvement.

Kaizen philosophy also finds a profound and natural application in personal improvement. I'll tell you more about it in the rest of the discussion.

**Kaizen and change.**

I am firmly convinced that the basis of everything is that success comes from change.

What drives you to change? The willingness to improve and solve the problems you have in your life.

As Dr. Robert Maurer, a great supporter of the Kaizen philosophy said:

In any area of your life, success results from how you collect your minutes. Thanks to thousands of small and frequent victories, a great goal can only be achieved.

The small victories each day give you the strength to continue and keep you focused on your goals.

Setting goals that are too big or upsetting your life in a too radical way generates a sense of fear in you and makes you fear failing in your intent, whatever results you want to achieve. But if these goals are broken down into smaller, more straightforward tasks, the road ahead will simply seem less steep.

All your successes are the result of small actions perpetrated over time. If your relationship is going well, for example, you make small gestures for your partner every day. This person's feeling towards you is the incremental result of a series of small actions, gestures, and emotions generated over time.

Like any other passion, love is not something that works in an " < UNK> < UNK> / off" ay. Thanks to small, simple, but essential gestures, it takes time to evolve and grow every day.

Kaizen method fits into this key: introduce small changes into your life. They will seem irrelevant to you, but if you stay consistent with them for a long enough period, one day, you will look back and be amazed at how far you have come.

So let's analyze how you can concretely apply the Kaizen method to your improvement.

Below I will walk you through a linear process for implementing continuous improvement in your life. Let's see it step by step:

-Decide What You Want to Become: The first step in introducing Kaizen into your life is deciding your goals. Now, I'm not saying this is simple—quite the contrary. Suppose you are among those who are undecided on the way to go. Determining your goals is the basis for all forms of personal growth and improvement. Knowing your dreams, or what can make you happy, means knowing in which areas to work to achieve them;

-Among all your goals, choose only one: once you have written down your goals, you will have to go and select only one. Even though this isn't easy, I know the Kaizen method was designed and works best by working on one area of your life at a time. For example, choose the goal that, if achieved, would have the most significant benefits for you. You will undoubtedly have time in the future to work in other areas of your life;

-Write a list of why this goal is not already part of your reality: once you have chosen the plan to work on, it is time to make a list of why it has not yet been achieved. What obstacles are you facing? You can start with the smallest of these, trying to remove them one by one. If you don't know what the cause is blocking you, you can think backward. I will explain this regard with an example. Let's say you have a huge goal to lose weight. For what reasons is this goal not already part of your reality? For example, you might reply that you haven't had the strength to play sports lately at the end of the day because, at that time, you are tired, and your willpower is very low. If so, a solution might be to wake up in the morning and work out when you are at the top of your energy.

I want to clarify that proposing a goal does not make you achieve the result. Once you understand how to act, you will have to stay true to what you promised yourself and work steadily to reach your goal.

Going back to the example, you could, for example, aim to lose 4 pounds in a month. The extent of how much you want to lose weight must be commensurate with your initial fitness and the amount of work you want to throw into that activity, about a month of work.

### The prodigious effects of the Kaizen method on your life

It remains only to illustrate the benefits you can obtain by applying the kaizen method to your life. Let's see the four main ones:

Train your mind: through the systematic use of the kaizen philosophy in your life, you will train your mind for success. You will always be projected towards the next step with the desire to improve continuously;

Gives you time to develop new skills: Based on introducing minor, slow improvements into your life, the kaizen method gives you the time to develop the skills you need to make that leap. Improving takes time and constant work. It is the small but frequent doses of commitment that make the difference in the long run;

Eliminate the sense of blocking you have in front of big goals: by introducing small and gradual improvements in your life, you will not experience that blockage that occurs when faced with significant challenges. One step at a time, without causing too much effort and stress;

It puts you in the perspective of having a purpose: by choosing the aspect of life to work on from time to time, you will feel immersed in your path to success and happiness. You will frame every little step you take in a much broader perspective, and for this reason, it will take on even more importance and meaning.

# CHAPTER 4
# FORGET ABOUT YOURSELF.

It is the pillar that connects to our inner child: when children focus on a game or activity that interests them, they forget about themselves and are entirely in the here and now. And we adults, too, if we are deeply immersed in a sensory experience that gives us pleasure, we end up forgetting ourselves; we are engaged in the flow, lightened by the weight of the Ego. This happens in front of Beauty, whatever form it takes for us: a painting, music, a natural spectacle, a leaf, an exquisitely crafted ceramic cup, a damask velvet, a wine. We enter a state of flow even when we work on something that interests us deeply, where we are no longer in charge but the work we are doing at that exact moment. By maintaining that flow and getting rid of the ego burden, the results will benefit, and the quality of our work will only improve.

Forgetting about oneself also means being humble, no matter how great the awards received for the excellent work done. It means playing even if no one listens to us, painting even if no one will ever admire our paintings, cooking even if no one else will taste our delicacies, just because while we paint, cook and play, we are in the flow, and we feel good.

Forget about oneself, get back in touch with the senses, and with the pleasure of simple experiences, for example, rediscovering contact with nature.

Most adults are unaware that the reins of their lives are held in the hands of a wounded and forgotten inner child.

According to psychologists, reconnecting to this deep part allows us to rediscover creativity, enthusiasm, and confidence for the future.

The "Inner Child" phenomenon

Psychiatrist Carl Jung 1912, first described the symbolic figure of the Inner Child by coining the term "puer aeternum".

Over the years, psychology has developed this concept to become an integral part of modern therapies.

The healthy inner child has enthusiasm, creativity, and confidence and can express their emotions without fear.

However, most adults have a wounded inner child whose basic needs for care, unconditional love, and recognition were not met in childhood.

Primal injury is recorded in the brain as a traumatic event associated with an unpleasant emotion. The thoughts that arise from this and that accompany the entire development of the child are negative:

"I'm not enough, I don't deserve love; I'm wrong".

We try to repress the pain as we grow up, but life presents us with the same lesson until we learn it.

Childhood trauma is relived above all in emotional relationships.

It is hoped that the "ideal partner" will satisfy those needs that were denied long ago.

It's impossible

Also, on the other side, there is often another injured child. Accusing each other thus becomes a defensive system in order not to come into contact with one's suffering.

Accept the past

This pain is in the past but must be faced and accepted in the present. Avoiding one's suffering only means prolonging it over time.

To become an adult, you have to "bite the bullet": infantile needs have not been satisfied by those who should have done so, and they never will be. We look after our inner child as a loving and understanding parents.

Contact the forgotten inner child.

The experts then offer some advice:

Having the courage to recognize the pain within oneself;

Searching for childhood memories;

Visualization exercises and guided meditations;

Doing activities that you loved in childhood;

Talking or writing to your inner child;

Relying on a therapist.

As the inner child gains confidence in his "new parent," the resistance will decrease.

The adult will have access to the purest and most spontaneous part of their childhood, such as creativity and enthusiasm for life. He will learn to live and enjoy the present just like a child. These positive emotions will also be reflected in external situations, including relationships that will be healthier and more fulfilling.

But the inner child has another secret: that unique and special talent that, for many, has become just a dream in the drawer. Who knows if it can finally turn into reality with the newfound creativity and lightheartedness?

The inner child knows how to forget about himself.

And this is a fundamental pillar to achieving one's ikigai.

According to this pillar, when we are focused and immersed in doing something we like, we forget everything around us, even ourselves.

Forgetting about ourselves helps us control our ego and put passion and love into everything we do without the constant thought of having recognition or reward in return.

This leads us in the flow to a state of grace in which we manage to get lost and practice activity for an indefinite time without realizing it.

# CHAPTER 5

# THE STATE OF FLOW

What is (and how to reach) the "state of flow" that makes you attentive and involved in any activity.

You know that feeling that time has flown? It is a scientific question that has to do with our skills, as the Hungarian psychologist Mihaly pointed out Csíkszentmihályi. We find ourselves in what Csíkszentmihályi calls a "state of flow," or a state of flow in which we are deeply immersed in what we are dedicating ourselves to, immune to most distractions, and time passes without we realize it. We have all experienced this feeling while skiing down a steep descent, trying to finish a book late at night, or perhaps during an after-dinner at a friend's house. Understanding how this happens helps us make every activity we dedicate ourselves to engaging.

## How the flow state is generated

The state of flow is connected to our level of intention. Csíkszentmihályi defines intent as focusing our attention on an action or goal. This happens when we spend more time than expected completing a task without taking it.

Consequently, it is directly proportional to the commitment and difficulty that an action or goal requires. When skiing down a steep descent, we need our full attention to avoid falling. When we continue to devour the pages of a book late at night, we want at all costs to know how the story ends. And after dinner at a friend's house, it's easy to be late when we're involved in an important argument or a game where everyone wants to win. In these cases, time does not represent a variable that we consider. This is because we are fully involved, we need all our skills, and the goal to be achieved is challenging at the right point.

When we deal with activities that do not require our commitment and are not challenging to complete,

as happens to those looking for something to see on TV, we are apathetic, devoid of interest and attention to what we are doing. On the other hand, if we have to work hard to reach a goal beyond our reach, as during copy and paste operations, we get bored. However, if our skills are all necessary, then we are relaxed because it is true that we must commit ourselves, but we are aware that we will achieve the surplus result.

On the other hand, when we do not have the necessary skills to achieve the goal we have set ourselves or have assigned, we worry, and worry becomes anxiety if the task is far from our reach.

To find the state of flow, we have two ways. One leads us to increase the difficulty of the activity we are dedicating ourselves to when it is too simple, thus transforming it into a challenge. If our skills are all needed, the more we raise the bar, the more we feel in control of the situation. The more the challenge becomes complex and the less predictable the result, we reach the state of flow. This is what the skier does when he chooses to turn tighter and tighter, the reader who decides to get to the end of the book instead of turning off the light, or friends who start a game of Risk after dinner.

The other way to reach that state where we are so involved that we lose track of time is to add skills to the ones we need. This allows us to move from the anxiety of not having the required skills to the excitement that we generate challenges not really within our reach. And the more the demand for our skills increases, the more we are in a flow state. This happens to the skier who wants to learn to jump, the reader who claims to memorize the fundamental concepts of a text lying in his bed late at night, or the group of friends discussing politics.

You enter the flow whenever you lose track of time by doing something challenging and exciting.

Mihaly Csikszentmihalyi, the "father" of the concept of the State of Flow (or the State of Flow), describes it as the moment in which the mind and body, totally absorbed in a given action, enter a condition of harmonic concentration.

Those who experience it feel entirely taken by an activity that drags them like a current.

Suddenly, the outside world ceases to exist.

Noises cease. External pressures cease.

There are no more distractions, no negative thoughts.

There are no other urgencies.

It is impossible to devote oneself to anything else because that activity completely captivates us, and we ride the moment. We dominate it.

We feel carried away by a positive, powerful, but friendly force, which allows us to reach unexpected goals and broaden our consciousness and knowledge.

In this original state of grace, we feel more than alive.

We are happy; we are excellent. In short, we are ecstatic.

We feel satisfaction and pleasure from the action itself, not from expectations, results, or back thoughts.

Finally, we get our best results in this state of flow.

This can be: an exceptional physical performance (in this case, we speak specifically of competitive trance), of superb writing, of a speech that amazes everyone.

Flow can therefore be experienced in different areas of life.

On the contrary, to live a happy life and satisfy one's need for self-realization, one should aim to experience it in as many areas as possible.

The flow state has six specific characteristics, and 3 are the requirements to achieve it.

When it comes to the Status of Flow, there is a lot of confusion.

Some confuse this specific state of mind with simple concentration, and some even with meditation.

In reality, as mentioned, the State of Flow has particular characteristics: knowing them will help you experience it as soon as possible (and as often as possible).

Let's see them.

1. Union between action and conscience

The action we perform in Flow State is:

- natural

- fluid

- authentic

- instinctive

There is no effort. There is no programming. Our consciousness becomes one with what we do. We are pure action.

2. Total absence of distractions

When we try to focus, we must actively strive to eliminate distractions.

Conversely, when we enter the Flow State, we are so engrossed that we ignore any distractions.

The difference is subtle but substantial.

3. Calm control

There is no trace of worries or anxieties.

We are not afraid of making mistakes and making a wrong impression. We are fine, calm, and confident.

This happens because the mind, totally enraptured in the present moment, calms the continuous inner chatter that usually accompanies us: we stop thinking and limit ourselves to being and doing.

4. Absence of judgment and loss of self-awareness

When we enter the flow state of mind, our thoughts are fearful and filled with judgment and criticism.

Pervaded by this mental silence, we lose consciousness of ourselves.

No, don't worry, no fainting!

You will be more present than ever: you will be immersed body and soul in action, and for a few minutes, you will forget about the fantasy film in which your mind is constantly trapped.

5. Destructuring of time

We don't know how long this experience lasts when we enter the flow.

This is, in fact, one of the most typical and, in some ways, curious signals of Flow: we perceive time in an altered way; depending on the action, the minutes seem to pass slower or faster, but always positively and pleasantly.

6. Autotelic experience

The pleasure we feel in doing what has absorbed us is pure, independent of further rewards and recognition.

We carried out that action driven by our deep will, not moved by a sense of duty or future expectations. This is why Flow is one of the most effective ways to cultivate our happiness.

There are no magic spells or disposable tricks to reach Flow State.

Indeed, the state of perennial inattention to which the "Dictatorship of the Smartphone has reduced us" makes it almost impossible for us to experience this peculiar psychological state (think of how many times you have become distracted by reading this chapter of just over 1,000 words ... if you are got here!)

But not all hope is lost.

We can recreate in our days what is the most fertile ground for this mental state to flourish, respecting these three requirements.

The three requirements of the State of Flow

A) Clear objectives

I will never tire of repeating it: learn to give yourself relevant, specific, and ambitious goals.

We can only find Flow by doing something that interests us, is clear to us, and challenges us.

And this last feature of our goals is significant; in fact, the second requirement to create the fertile ground for the Flow State is

B) Balance between the difficulties to be faced and our skills. Simple activities that do not test our skills lead us to feel apathy.

In dealing with too simple activities, we feel relaxed but also bored.

If we do not have the necessary skills to complete specific actions, we feel stressed.

We aspire to enter the State of Flow by finding the right balance between difficulty and a sense of mastery.

C) Immediate and specific feedback

Whether they are internal, I.E., emotions or signals from the body, or external, feedbacks indicate how we are working towards our goal and function as positive reinforcers.

The activities that bring us to the State of Flow give us immediate and specific feedback.

In short, the more we act, the more we feel good, satisfied, and competent.

These are the three basic requirements to enter the Flow State.

Knowing them will help you cultivate them. About that

We close this chapter by launching you two challenges:

What hobby, sport, or activity made you experience the Flow State as I have described it to you? If you've spotted it, think about how to spend more time on it this week.

How can you change the way you work or study to turn your schedule into opportunities to enter Flow State as often?

# CHAPTER 6

# THE JOY OF LITTLE THINGS

There will come a day when, almost by chance, we realize that it's the little things that make sense of everything else. We have neglected the same ones due to lack of time, so busy with personal and professional affairs that we cannot give them the right weight. And they were always there, in the only place where we didn't look.

Yet those are the things that are still worth wondering about, for which to smile every morning despite the hostile wind, those that give us the strength to start over after each fall. But the frenzy, the speed so high that it marks our days, has led us to neglect them, but it is not too late to enjoy all the joy they can give.

Because once the smartphone is removed and the computer turned off, all we have left are fragments of time that fly without us realizing it. And they are too short of learning how wonderful it is to get lost in the smiles of a child, in the stories of a wise older man, or in the infinite horizon, beyond the sea.

An inability to appreciate the little things that have crept into our lives made us lose so much, but let's remember that nothing is lost. But stop, and take some time for us, to realize that those things we have taken for granted are still there.

So let's do it; let's stop and learn to marvel in their presence, to savor the amazement of these little things that represent the true essence of life—a goodnight kiss, a lonely sunset, a starry sky to admire with those we love. Small daily joys give us the energy to face that path called life.

Let's promise not to do it again, not to neglect those sunny days, not to get lost among the thousands of commitments for their own sake, and on the contrary, to spend time with those we love, to give a gift to those who fill our life, to read a book, to caress our pet, to hug a friend and celebrate the changing seasons because it is behind all this that the most authentic happiness is hidden.

Ingratitude makes you blind, while being grateful for life pays off. According to research by the University of Notre Dame (Indiana), those who want to excel at all costs risk spending their lives trying to reach an increasingly distant and difficult goal, missing out on the charm and beauty of the here and now. Research participants thirsting for fame complained about an unfulfilling life. The unbridled ambition made them insatiable: even those who had obtained a university chair were disappointed because they considered themselves worthy of a Nobel Prize. The risk is to develop a strict severity towards oneself that does not foresee the possibility of falling, being tired, or needing to take a rest.

Hofstra psychologists University of Hempstead (New York) found that people aware of what they have and happy to have it have a better life in many ways. They have better social relationships; they do not envy those who have more, and they are more optimistic and well disposed towards others. From a neurobiological point of view, a satisfied brain produces substances, such as neurotransmitters and hormones, which positively reinforce mood and health. Whenever we are happy, the brain receives positive feedback, as if we were telling it: "I am informing you that I am happy." If we get used to appreciating what we have, we will have a fuller, more fortunate, and richer perception of life. Could it be the kiss of luck that brings joy? Too easy. The opposite is demonstrated by another work, this time by the University of California, which explains how the inner predisposition to satisfaction and contentment attracts the positive influences of life and not vice versa. The proof is that these people do not lose their smiles when everything goes wrong, always managing to see the glass half full. The reason? Gratitude reduces stress by fueling positive thoughts. It should be cultivated with care and watered every day like a plant in the garden. If it withers, we will no longer be able to appreciate even the smile of a grandchild, the compliments of a colleague, or the pleasure of an unexpected gift. The US magazine Forbes called it " drift syndrome," the inability to enjoy what surrounds us. A modern evil.

When happiness never comes.

Sunsets and spectacles of nature no longer enchant; at most, they are immortalized on the flat screen of the mobile phone. Pampering, little attention, and surprises do not melt the heart of those who always aim for something more. Everyday problems extinguish enthusiasm and prevent us from appreciating what beautiful happens to us. In the effort to "make ends meet," always be fit, and show off success, you lose the ability to take pleasure in what you are lucky enough to have already. Accustomed to the immediate satisfaction of desires, constantly connected and ready to instantly obtain any information, you live under the banner of "everything and now." This attitude contrasts with the natural mechanism of the mind, which needs time, the ability to wait and tolerate frustrations, to evolve. Furthermore, when nothing excites anymore, one can succumb to the temptation to obtain satisfaction artificially, with even dangerous habits (compulsive shopping, gambling) that "simulate" happiness in the brain center of gratification, providing immediate satisfaction but fleeting illusory.

Those satisfied enjoy, but being satisfied does not mean sitting down.

The context does not help because it mercilessly labels those who do not always expect the best. Social expectations and a culture marked by competition tend to judge those who live by being content negatively. Instead, this ability does not coincide with passivity or mediocrity. It doesn't mean giving up, wanting, or giving up on your dreams. It is not the antithesis of ambition, with the desire to improve, evolve, and fulfill ourselves. You can be proactive, determined, and combative but at the same time, be happy with what you have, even when life asks for some renunciation. So when is it correct and legitimate to stop and appreciate the moment? We are satisfied positively every time we reach a small goal; we give ourselves time to enjoy it and then move on to the next stage.

What pleases us today must be the starting point for what we want tomorrow. One of the secrets of longevity has recently been shown in always having desires and goals to achieve, without letting go passively to life as it flows. Therefore, being satisfied has a positive meaning when not always being unhappy or complaining about not having done enough. Still, it takes on a negative connotation when it is equivalent to not having goals to aim for.

Satisfied people enjoy it, but finding the right balance is not easy. One of the secrets is to give oneself achievable and not illusory goals and then aim gradually higher. Otherwise, you risk being disappointed when you fail to hit the target. Focusing on one step at a time gives you the proper enthusiasm and strength to move forward. Not all desires deserve to be pursued:

1.      Take an honest examination of yourself, analyze what you care about, and what makes your life fulfilling.

2.      Prioritize; choose what you want, need, and not what you would like to show others.

3.      Don't be selfish.

The quality of relationships is what fills an existence and gives it meaning. Narcissistically oriented perfectionism pushes you to consider only your own needs. The construction of a shared project is often more satisfying than individual and solitary goals. There are also two traps to stay clear of. The first is that of the " anticipation of desires." We satisfy needs even before expressing them: not cultivating the desire for things takes away the pleasure of earning them and enjoying them ». An example: the habit of "guessing" the ending of a film to demonstrate wit and intelligence only mortifies the fibrillation of expectation, reveals research from Ohio State University and the University of Hanover. The other is that of destructive confrontation. We stop believing that the lives of others and the successes of others are better than our own. Social media deceive us because they lead us to measure the degree of satisfaction of a person based on his public image. Those who are truly happy don't need to show it off.

A useful exercise

Write down three things about the day each night that made you happy. This exercise works because it teaches us to consider gratitude as a choice, a way of being. People are surprised at how much the days, even the "bad" ones, are full of reasons to rejoice: moments, dialogues, meetings, news, or events that, in the frenzy of the day, do not give importance. Does nothing come to mind? Think better. As Barry Schwartz writes in The Paradox of Choice, the list of gratitude most of the time does not include exceptional events but is made up of little things. Occasionally, the list consists of something striking, such as a promotion or a great first date.

# CHAPTER 7

# LIVE IN THE HERE AND NOW.

---

L ive the Present, without being trapped between past and future!" Horace, Carpe Diem.

The mind never stops.

Our mind, if left to itself, never stops. He constantly wanders among thoughts, memories, and projects over which we no longer have, or do not yet have, power and control.

We often mull over what it was:

" If I had chosen that faculty now I would have a job!";

" If I hadn't done that we'd probably still be together."

Other times we tend to worry excessively about what will be and to make plans for what our future will look like:

" I have to graduate within 25 years!";

" What will I do if at 30 I still don't have a family?".

These mental processes will always be mentally and emotionally, always elsewhere, never " here and now."

The "automatic pilot" is an obstacle to the "here and now."

Most of us live on "automatic pilot": our body is present, it does things unconsciously, but the mind is somewhere else. While we go about daily activities, our mind is rarely focused on what we are doing at that moment.

Watch your mobile while you eat.

I was humming while taking a shower.

These are examples of how our minds are often disconnected from our bodies and what we are doing. This happens because we leave the things we are used to doing and not needing particular attention at the mercy of an "automatic pilot."

It is an excellent obstacle to being aware, live, and enjoying what we are doing at the precise moment, we are doing it.

This can be changed through Mindfulness.

This concept has its roots in Buddhist contemplative traditions; the English name derives from the word sati, which in the Pali language means "awareness" or "present and active attention."

Mindfulness is paying attention to a particular thing, in a specific way, to the present moment and without judgment: knowing where our mind is and choosing where to direct it helps us live the "here and now" with awareness. Being a practice, Mindfulness needs to be cultivated with perseverance, time, and patience.

There are two ways of practicing Mindfulness: the formal and the informal.

Formal practice follows a defined program and consists of:

carve out some time every day to devote to meditation and silence;

pay attention to breathing, sounds, emotions, and senses.

The informal practice does not follow precise rules and consists of:

aware of everyday life;

Pay new attention to all the daily activities we usually carry out by activating the "autopilot," such as driving, eating, and walking.

Exercise: Mindfulness of the breath

To practice mindful breathing, follow these three steps:

1) FIND A QUIET PLACE

Choose a place where you are sure you will not be disturbed by the time it takes to practice.

2) FIND A COMFORTABLE LOCATION

You can sit on a chair or stay on the ground with your legs crossed, your back really straight, and your hands are resting on your legs.

3) CLOSE YOUR EYES AND PAY ATTENTION TO YOUR BREATH

Try to feel the breath and follow the sensations that accompany it. You can observe your breathing in various body parts: the nostrils, the chest, and the belly. I advise you to focus on the movement of the abdomen, which will swell with each inhalation and then deflate with each exhalation: the effect will be remarkably calming!

Breath advice

## ABANDON ALL ATTEMPTS TO CONTROL

Don't try to control your breathing; try to feel it flow from moment to moment, trying to follow its flow;

## SUSPEND THE JUDGMENT

If your mind moves away from the breath and starts wandering, know that this is a normal phenomenon, so don't judge yourself. When you realize it tries to understand where your mind has gone, observe what distracted it, and with kindness and delicacy, turn your attention back to the point of the body where you are following the breath and the sensations that accompany it;

## PRACTICE CONSTANTLY

Repeat the exercise several times a day.

Being here and now is a work of awareness that needs daily practice.

It is straightforward to be "prey" of thoughts and swing between the past and the future, searching for trouble.

Stay hooked on your body, your physicality, the energy you feel, and your breath. You are also your body, and it is alive and making itself felt right now.

Focus your attention on what your senses allow you to grasp at this moment through smells, sounds, tastes, and tactile sensations such as external perceptions on the skin, the wind in your hair, and the heat of the sun.

Become aware of the space you occupy, of your corporeality, of your movements and gestures, of your voice.

Allow yourself moments of silence in a secluded corner of the house where you listen only to your breath, letting your thoughts flow and disperse.

Let emptiness reign for a few minutes a day, the absence of thought.

Constant practice will make this easy and enjoyable. In the beginning, we don't know how to silence the internal dialogue, the ideas that flow, the mind that wanders, and everything can be challenging.

Don't give up.

# CHAPTER 8

# LIVING IN HARMONY

A nother pillar of the ikigai philosophy is to live in harmony. I am seeking balance and harmony in one's life.

The five qualities necessary to live in harmony with oneself.

**Fluidity means knowing how to adapt to any challenge life places us in front of.**

To be like water in its perennial flow; the water flows, creeps, always finds a way, bypasses every obstacle it encounters; it can neither be repressed nor compressed. Even if it is contained or contained, it always has its kinetic energy.

It is no coincidence that water is the essential element of nature; we are mainly composed of water!

Fears, feelings of guilt, anxiety, insecurities, and the need for control: are all elements that block the flow of our energy, and make us rigid, sometimes even paralyzed!

If we observe, the water in its journey always chooses the most straightforward path or the one where it meets the least resistance; we, on the other hand, very often complicate our lives by losing ourselves in absurd ways that we sometimes stubbornly want to follow, thus wasting a lot of energy.

What do we need to learn, then?

We learn to follow the flow of life without resisting, without rejecting what it offers us; if we rely on life, life itself will lead us exactly where we need to go. Life itself will find a way to get around obstacles and find another way.

But we have to get carried away.

If we remain rigid, it cannot lead us anywhere; we will never reach any goal if we get stuck!

**Sensitivity**

Sensitivity means realizing what is happening around us, learning to be receptive, and being able to pick up all those signals that life transmits to us and that we are too busy and distracted to receive!

Cultivating one's sensitivity means learning to use all our senses to the fullest of our potential, including the sixth sense, that voice of intuition that guides us in life.

It means training a vision of existence that is so deep and rooted, mature and aware, that every time we can elaborate new responses to the challenges that come our way, moving them to a higher, spiritual level.

It means knowing how to seek in everything, in every event, the hidden meaning, the opportunity for evolution and elevation.

Being sensitive means remaining alert, present, and attentive; it means looking at things from all points of view, going around them, and finding their hidden sides.

Sensitivity allows you to enjoy life to the fullest, to fully enjoy every sound, every scent, every gesture, every flavor, leaving a trace in your soul.

Being sensitive means learning to notice the miracles that happen to you every day; it means realizing that you are every instant a spectator of the magic of life in which we are called to participate.

**Freedom**

Freedom means allowing us to express our true nature.

Freedom is not understood as having a life devoid of duties or commitments. You can do whatever you want, but space is understood as allowing yourself the possibility of being what you are, always!

Freedom is understood as respect for oneself, one's perceptions, one's intuition, one's ideals, one's principles, one's feelings!

Being free means eliminating a thousand masks we wear every day to appear, for fear of judgment, to be accepted or well-liked, not to be abandoned, to please.

It means shaking off the conventions and beliefs that do not belong to us and suffocate us; it means building authentic relationships with others through which we can show ourselves, naked, precisely as we are!

You are free means always following your feelings, listening to your soul, and expressing your essence.

The conquest of this type of freedom will allow us to grant it to others without any judgment.

I am sure that everyone in this dimension has chosen his experience to get something out of it, to draw a lesson from it; let us, therefore, leave in peace what we are destined to meet on our path, allowing them to evolve according to their needs and their plans.

Just as we allow ourselves the freedom to experience the vicissitudes that our nature attracts to us, to enable us to progress.

**Opening the mind**

Opening the mind allows us to acquire wisdom.

We are eternal beings, and once we understand and accept this, we can allow ourselves to remain open to any experience, thought, practice or theory and then discern which one we want to make our own, accepting what resonates with our essence.

Learning not to judge keeps us open. When we define anything as of right or wrong, reasonable or unreasonable, positive or negative, we set limits, we put stakes, thus precluding ourselves from living experiences, encounters, or emotions that are our own. Nature has attracted us, but our limited ego rejects it out of fear or defense.

**Opening of the heart**

In addition to the mind, we must be able to open the heart to give breath to our soul; this means entering a dimension of collaboration concerning the world. It means allowing unlimited love to permeate our every moment, every experience, encounter, and gesture.

Love is the only real transforming force we have; it is what can allow us to overcome the phase in which we feel victims, the phase of accusation, and introduces us to a dimension where we are in love with ourselves for no reason, of life, of nature, of the people around us because everything becomes a beautiful expression of the miracle of existence.

It is what plunges us into pure joy, that which is felt in simple existence and which leads us beyond our earthly dimension.

Also, to live in harmony, remember to:

1- Always stay hooked on reality.

Please do not shy away from problems but face them with courage and confidence. Do what you can do, practical and immediate.

2- Cultivate a sense of beauty and sound.

Keeping a high profile keeps morale high, so it is essential to nurture the beauty and goodness in every activity and moment of the day.

3- Watch over the mind and emotions.

If they turn black to bring backlight, even thinking about things or people we particularly like (even frivolous things are acceptable).

4- Remember to dream.

Dreams contain desires. Good wishes are motivating. Listen to your goals and know in depth what you want!

5- Make practical plans.

After dreaming, develop your dream into a practical plan, and see where the program takes you. It's a great way to keep your mind active and get things done.

6- Take care of others.

You will do something good and move from a static position. Often dedicating oneself to others also leads to solutions to one's problems. Treat people who are intimate with us. Always improve relationships. To transmit love on every occasion to everyone.

7- Feeding your Soul.

Reading good books, finding new things to do, and practicing some art are some of the ways to cultivate your Soul.

8- Make even short forays into nature.

Admire a landscape, the starry sky, a flower, a cloud. Everything reconnects because the vibrations of nature are powerful and rebalancing.

9- Alternate with balance rest and activity and do meditation.

You need to recharge and discharge your energy during the day.

10- Take care of your body.

Express love for yourself with attention to the body, to its basic needs: to eat, rest, and natural beauty treatments, all seasoned with optimism and lack of criticism. In this way, you stay in shape and feel better psychologically too.

# CHAPTER 9

# HOW TO FIND YOUR IKIGAI

I t is difficult to feel fulfilled in Life, especially at work.

Finding the right job can be a real headache for most people and is often a much more complex search than you think.

The word "work" in some languages becomes "fatigue" or "labor," not exactly the most encouraging thing in the world!

However, thinkers and philosophers throughout history have seen work as a way to thrive.

The profession one practices result from many variables and, in particular, choosing to invest in a specific field. Today it is widespread to change one's path, professional orientation during one's career, or even reorient oneself during one's studies.

The IKIGAI method is inspired by a Japanese philosophy that allows you to find your career orientation and path. IKIGAI means "reason to be" or "joy of living."

STEP ONE ASK WHAT YOU LIKE

This step seems very simple, but it requires honest introspection. You can start with the following question: what do I like to do in my free time?

Some activities make time go by so quickly that we don't realize it. It is about identifying what makes us truly happy. Activities we are passionate about It can be contacted with others, an artistic practice, sport, or even a love of rhetoric. Whoever wants to be always correct will know what we are talking about!

Ask those around you for advice as it can be of great help. The people around us know us well and can sometimes identify something evident that we cannot see. We can ask them what they think are our qualities and strengths, essential elements for a successful career.

SECOND STEP. WHAT CAN YOU DO?

Starting with a topic that you already know can be an effective strategy to begin well, and, as the saying goes, those who start well are already half the battle. Starting with something we already know how to do, pushes us to believe in ourselves, giving us the right motivation to go on and not give up when the first difficulties arrive because "if I succeeded yesterday, I could do it today!". In addition, it makes us want to improve ourselves more and more and, above all, to learn new things.

What about what you don't know how to do yet? Practice! Brazilian writer Paulo Coelho states that "there is only one way to learn: through action."

Only through experience can we know what suits us, what motivates us, and what we like to do. To gain experience, we can consider internships, fixed-term contracts, or training. Professional experience is a kind of life-size orientation test!

The mental state is also critical. Young people are often stressed about choosing their career orientation. To understand which job we like we need to practice.

Suppose you cannot access an internship, thanks to the interconnected world we live in. In that case, you can virtually meet (on LinkedIn, in Facebook groups ...) with professionals who attract your attention to learn about their experiences. And don't forget your network of friends and acquaintances!

THIRD STEP. ASK YOURSELF: "WHAT DOES THE WORLD NEED?"

This question is helpful because, on the one hand, it allows us to go deeper and make even more clarity. Knowing that we are doing a job with a social, environmental value, etc., we would more likely feel balanced with ourselves and motivated.

Let's take the current situation, for example. The pandemic caused by the new Coronavirus Sars-Nov-2 ( Covid 19) has increased the need for professionals in the health field and factory workers to produce masks. Looking at what is happening and asking yourself about the required professions can help you on the right path.

The combo "what you like to do" and "what the world needs" can, for example, lead a person who likes to travel and at the same time is sensitive to the issue of human rights to do the job of a cultural mediator.

FOURTH STEP. KEEP UP TO DATE ON THE LABOR MARKET AND ASK YOURSELF: "WHAT COULD I BE PAID FOR?"

We know money is essential to living and afford the things we like to do.

It is essential for these three reasons:

First, labor market variables are fundamental in choosing a profession (hiring rate, level of education required, etc.).

Second, because it can give you ideas or ideas about a job you don't yet know.

And finally, this is an excellent test of orientation and motivation.

Let's take the example of Marta, an eighteen-year-old who would like to be a journalist. By inquiring about this profession, he realizes that the demand is very high, but he also discovered many other related disciplines, especially digital ones, such as online communication. Her motivation to become a journalist persists; despite all the information that it is tough to find a job in this field, Marta chooses the digital path.

Furthermore, with good information, you will be able to discover other professions related to the one you are interested in, which may better suit your profile.

In short, we can only encourage your curiosity: by searching and digging deep, we can find natural treasures.

Reflecting on career guidance can take time. Each new step

allows you to get closer to the right direction. It is about not losing patience and perseverance. As Albert Einstein used to say: "Life is like riding a bicycle. You have to keep going in order not to lose your balance."

Get inspired by successful people (which I remind you is the past participle of happening) and unleash your mind.

## CHANGE MENTALITY

Stop complaining and just look at the negative !. Remember that crises have always existed in human Life, and often this word etymologically had a positive connotation (including in ancient Greek, in which etymologically crisis (crino) meant "change," "detachment from the past").

## SET A GOAL

Who does not get anywhere lives with a "life of chance," ergo takes what arrives? Start thinking about what your outlets might be and start setting attainable goals.

## MANAGE YOUR PASSION

Whatever your passion is, see immediately in which sectors you can apply it to and how you can use your talent. You may have to compromise to "start the wrong way," but if you manage to create an opening, you will have the basis for doing what you want over time. The web offers a lot of possibilities to start through new channels or sectors that come close to yours.

Often, those who would like to become an illustrator begin by being a graphic designer, dealing with the web or layout, which is perhaps less attractive in their opinion. Over time, however, he manages to create the foundations to be known and takes illustrated photos or accurate advertising illustrations.

ENJOY THE ROUTE

Don't be in a hurry. Successful people always declare that the best part of their journey has been the path.

WORK AND PASSION BECOME CONCILIATED ONLY IF YOU WANT TO

If you resign yourself from the beginning to the first obstacle, you do not believe in it. I advise you, especially initially, to create a valid alternative. Look for a part-time job or something to help you supplement. The important thing is not to focus everything on your goal because the obsession will make you feel even worse, and therefore, over time, you will exasperate yourself, and you will end up failing. Put yourself in a position to say: what do I have to lose?

# CHAPTER 10

# WABI-SABI

---

Wabi-sabi is the imperfection that becomes perfection.

In the Japanese language, some words cannot be easily translated...

Here is an example: wabi-sabi

Two characters:侘( Wabi ) and 寂(Sabi), the union of two words with a single meaning that defines a vision of the world that becomes art.

Wabi-sabi has its roots in accepting the transience of things and the imperfection that derives from it, a natural weakness due to the inevitable passage of time.

The term Sabi has to do with transience, the authenticity of age that becomes beauty.

Practicing Sabi means learning to accept the natural cycle of growth, death, and the imperfections that accompany this progression.Combining these two words aims to create a feeling that finds harmony in nature and simple living with little.

An example of wabi-sabi is Hagi pottery, the Japanese pottery used in many tea ceremonies. The pieces are often rustic and straightforward, with asymmetrical shapes and raw style. The wear and tear and its actual age give the object a unique beauty to be contemplated. Wabi-sabi nature and the inevitability of time teach us the art of living. We must strip ourselves of the extra to enrich ourselves with simplicity, without glories or redundancies. If well kept and recovered, natural materials and basic things give charm and immortality.

Wabi-Sabi is a cardinal principle of the Japanese worldview. Its resilience is the capacity to accept our fragility, imperfection, and transience. Wabi-Sabi is also essentiality, maximum simplicity, and the extreme synthesis of every form.

Appropriating this lifestyle now appears to be a requirement in our culture, characterized by fear, individualism, a need for control, and frustration. And it represents an opportunity for modern man to develop a new method of poetic thought, comprehend the beauty and complexities of reality, and feel at one with it.

What is Wabi-Sabi, exactly? « Wabi is melancholy, sweet sadness, evaporation, and imperfection. Sabi is the passage of time, that which disappears and never returns. In a nutshell, this is happiness.

Therefore, a slower pace of Life allows us to notice the little things. You discover the universe's rhythm in the slowness, become aware, and taste the experience until the end because you are there. Projecting oneself into the future is frequently the source of deep dissatisfaction and anxiety. We never seem to be, never do enough. OMI is a

simple practice ( One Minute Immersion). It is a one-minute

mindfulness or awareness practice repeated several times (at least twice) throughout the day. Here's how to go about it: Consider an imperfect aspect of your Life or body while sitting with your spine straight. Consider this flaw to be a spirit, an invisible but sentient presence. Place your left hand gently on your mouth and nose. Finally, he says, "I have faith in you!" into the cup formed by the hollow of your hand. This is linked to understanding nature's language and wabi-sabi: balance, moderation, and temperance.

The second ritual is letting go, also known as "too-mo-and-do." You can make something even more appealing than what you're doing. You must make room, believe in your destiny, be creative, nurture more significant projects, and look a little further ahead.

Keep as much nostalgia for what has passed as possible. Wabi-sabi is fundamentally about nostalgia. It's a work of poetry. It is beauty capable of heightening your sensitivity and creativity and fostering your ever-expanding visions.

Make a natural object, such as a pebble, a pine cone, a leaf, a sprig, an apple, a tomato, or a handful of rice grains, the symbol of something you can let go of to overcome yourself. To generate new ideas and free up energy for new endeavors.

Place this item in a special location in your home for seven days. Before you go to bed, visualize the object and consider what you need to let go of in the evening. Do not use the mind to calculate or analyze because the mind can demonstrate everything and the opposite of everything simultaneously. If it is animated by huge fear, it will make it difficult for you to let go of the old aspects of your life to make room for the new.

It is preferable to perceive rather than think; feel the infinite possibilities that will open up to you once you have cleared the way for the new, letting go of the ballast.

# CHAPTER 11

# METAPHOR AND TECHNIQUE OF KINTSUGI: THE ART OF PRECIOUS SCARS

---

Japan is a country that has given the world countless and often unique skills. Among these, we find Ikebana, the art of floral composition, or Shodō, the art of calligraphy.

In this chapter, we focus on art that represents a beautiful metaphor for the concept of resilience, namely the Kintsugi (pronounced: chinzughi ). This ancient technique replaces broken pottery and ceramics by applying lacquers mixed with precious metal powders, such as gold and silver, by being inserted between the cracks or molding them into the shape of the missing piece.

Kintsugi artisans are rare outside of Japan, as the method used is much older than one might believe.

The word " kintsugi " is written with kanji 金継ぎ, which respectively mean "gold" (金) and "fix" (継ぎ). We can translate it as "fix with gold" or even "golden patch." Sometimes, especially in the West, you can also meet the name of Kintsukuroi, written with kanji 金繕い and translated as "gold" and "repairer" (繕い), hence "repairer who uses gold."

This art is much older than one might believe: Japanese pottery's first rudimentary repair techniques date back to the Jomon period, a vast era from 10,000 BC to 400 BC. Finds of the oldest pottery in the world are now kept in museums in Tokyo.

As an art form, it began to evolve in the 15th century, during the Muromachi period (1336 - 1573): a legend has it that the Shogun (the highest possible military title) Ashikaga Yoshimasa, after his favorite teacup broke, then commissioned artisans to repair it so that it was still usable and worthy of its office. The artisans used natural lacquer mixed with gold dust to succeed in the enterprise, obtaining a fantastic result from an artistic and artisan (and functional) point of view.

The success of this new form of craftsmanship took hold very quickly among the courts and collectors of the time: there were numerous cases of porcelain voluntarily broken to ensure that they were repaired using the Kintsugi technique, increasing their economic and artistic value.

Each object repaired with this technique becomes one of a kind. It will never be possible to break two pieces identically. The final result, after being fixed, will always be a unique piece of art in the world.

**Techniques**

Kintsugi's techniques can be summarized in a very simplistic way, grouping them into three categories:

Hibi (ひ び) or "crack," where superficial cracks are repaired.

Kake no Kintsugi Rei (欠 け の 金 継 ぎ 例), or "example of golden repair (of the missing piece)," in which the missing piece is made to measure, made entirely of lacquer and gold.

Yobitsugi (呼 び 継 ぎ) or "invitation to mend/unite," where a piece from another very similar porcelain is used, but not the original one.

**The philosophical aspect**

The appeal of this repair technique goes beyond the beauty of the precious material used, be it gold, silver, or platinum.

The Kintsugi has a solid philosophical value for the artisans who repair and those who witness the process or receive the repaired object. A repair is a powerful form of psychological therapy, as we transfer a possible adverse event in our Life onto the broken object. Once fixed, it will be as if we were able to select a small part of what we suffered from the negative. Kintsugi is often associated with resilience, the ability to always get up after a fall.

Making a simple comparison, we can think of our Life as a handcrafted teacup: each one is unique in the world since each artisan has a unique hand. However similar two pieces are, they will never be completely identical.

Yet our Life is not static like a cup: we move, live, love, hate, suffer and get up. Each of these actions can reinvigorate the strength of our cup, or it can break it, more or less severely. We can suffer physical wounds but also (and above all) emotional wounds. Each affects us more or less deeply, leaving signs that sometimes accompany us throughout Life.

## The importance of scars

Despite everything that can happen to us, we get back on our feet and continue to live. So we choose to "repair" these wounds or let time heal them for us. Every time a wound closes, it leaves a scar.

The spiritual meaning of Kintsugi lies precisely in this aspect: we must not hide the wounds we have or be ashamed of them because if we "repair" them in the right way, that is by overcoming the trauma they left us and learning from it, they will become medals, trophies that celebrate the battles we survived.

How to heal from this wound is up to us: if we let it settle passively, continuing to suffer from the pain caused, then we will have a rudimentary repair (like those of the Jomon period ), but if instead, we know how to get up again, even slowly, but with the pride in having succeeded in overcoming the problem, then the work will in effect be a golden repair worthy of the Shogun.

Every wound we carry tells us who we are, where we come from, what we have endured to date, and how we got out of it. It will be our very personal Kintsugi art. A shiny golden scar closed to perfection.

## Beauty in impermanence

A vision belonging to Zen Buddhism is called Wabi-sabi and sinks its principles into Kintsugi: this vision enhances the beauty of imperfection and ephemeral, that is, "nothing is eternal." Despite the inevitability of all things, there is a profound beauty in their impermanence, in the fact that they will not remain as they are forever.

In the repaired object, we see this ephemeral beauty enhanced as it is recomposed more beautifully.

This is the Japanese art of accepting damage: we cannot erase what has been. Crying will not restore our teacup to the way it was before. However, if we collect the pieces and roll up our sleeves, we will be able to repair them and make them more beautiful than before, but this will never be possible if we do not first accept what it was.

Everything is up to us and how we decide to face Life'sLife's problems and turn them into growth opportunities. From the greatest tragedies to the most insignificant trifles, we have the extraordinary power to rise more robust than before.

In Japanese, there is a word that is very suitable for this concept, but it does not have a precise translation in our language: shouganai (しょうがない). It can be used in various forms and ways, but the meaning that interests us is to accept something that, however tiring or dull, we cannot avoid. Once again, taking the "damage" for what it is, solving it in the best possible way, and welcoming it as a precious life lesson that will make our cracks even more special.

# CHAPTER 12

# OKINAWA AND ITS SECRETS

H ARA HACHI BU" is the principle on which the people of Okinawa base their diet.

Means EAT UP TO 80% SATIETH.

They enjoy the highest healthy life expectancy and one of the highest percentages of centenarians. Furthermore, the inhabitants of Okinawans get fewer diseases from cancer and cardiovascular disorders than Americans compared the Japanese people.

The scientific literature powerfully highlights how eating too much badly puts us at a very high risk for our health by decreasing the duration of our Life. Some studies published in Science and Nature confirm that the secret to a long healthy life lies in a frugal attitude at the table. A molecule (Creb1) has recently been identified that protects neurons from aging and is activated precisely if you eat less. This molecule lights up following a low-calorie diet and activates genes that are important for longevity and good brain function.

Never as in this historical period has there been so much talk of healthy nutrition, longevity, and health, and never have there been so many "theories" on achieving healthy longevity.

Yet there are some peoples in the world who, unaware of everything the leading nutrition experts say, are well over 100 years of age. They are the centenarians of the Blue Zones of the world. Therefore, we are talking about five areas observed by numerous scholars: Sardinia in Italy, Okinawa Island in Japan, Seventh-day Adventists in California ( Loma Linda ), Nicoya in Costa Rica, and the island of Ikaria in Greece.

The island of Okinawa, Japan, was the first area to be studied.

THE INHABITANTS OF OKINAWA

Okinawans enjoy the highest healthy life expectancy and one of the highest percentages of centenarians. Life expectancy is 78 years for men and 86 for women. In 2007 the number of centenarians was 457 or 35 for every 100 inhabitants. But most sensational is the low incidence of diseases such as diabetes, stroke, Alzheimer's, and obesity to which this population appears to be immune.

In addition to maintaining optimal health, Okinawan centenarians maintain physical strength and energy that today's 20-year-olds envy.

According to the studies carried out by Dan Buettner, explorer and writer who has studied at length the lifestyle habits of Okinawa's centenarians, several fundamental aspects must be considered.

These people had to face a tough life during the war, where food was scarce and water was very little. They managed to eat sweet potatoes (even three times a day) and rarely some fish. Once a year, they managed to slaughter the family pig and thus consumed the meat. However, they were usually constantly hungry.

After the war, the eating style of the Okinawan people remained predominantly vegetarian, with regular consumption of fruits, vegetables, soy, seaweed, and lots of fish.

The algae used and the fish are known for their high content of Omega-3 essential fatty acids, which play a crucial role in modulating the game of inflammation at all levels of the body.

OMEGA-3 AND LONGEVITY

Omega-3 essential fatty acids are divided into two groups: ALA (α-linoleic acid) contained in foods of plant origin, such as walnuts, flax seeds, and soya, and long-lasting EPA and DHA chain ( eicosapentaenoic and docosahexaenoic acid ), mainly contained in fish. The fish richest in Omega-3 are fresh tuna, salmon, mackerel, eel, sardine, and herring.

Large fish have a high mercury content, so it is preferable to prefer small fish.

Greenlight for mackerel, anchovies, sardines, and herring !!

The type of cooking to be used is also essential.

All cooking causes minimal Omega-3 loss. The few types of research carried out so far have shown that steaming and grilling for no more than 15 minutes are the best in the case of sea bream. With this method, the loss of Omega-3 varies from 4 to 25%. As for salmon, it has been seen that both in frying (6 minutes) and steam (12 minutes), the loss of Omega-3 is almost zero.

Omega-3 and six fatty acids are fundamental components of

plasma membranes, and their metabolic transformation gives rise to eicosanoids, essential mediators of numerous cellular reactions. They modulate each other, and the proper Omega-6 / Omega-3 ratio should be between 1: 1 or 3: 1.

The long-lived Japanese have a ratio of 1.5: 1, while the Americans have a 15: 1. An excessive amount of Omega-6 and a diet with a high glycemic index can trigger cellular inflammations with a consequent risk of developing numerous diseases.

This means that we eat very severely and that the favorite foods, especially among young people, are industrial fries, snacks full of sugars, fats, and salt.

HOW TO ENSURE THE RIGHT AMOUNT OF OMEGA-3

Here's what we should do to ensure we have the right balance between Omega-6 and Omega-3!

We eat fish at least 3-4 times a week, preferring the varieties listed above, in the quantities indicated in the LARN IV: (Fresh/frozen fish, mollusks and crustaceans 150 gr, Preserved fish, mollusks, and crustaceans 50 gr)

We increase the consumption of nuts such as walnuts, hazelnuts, and almonds, even 20 to 30 grams per day.

We limit the content of foods rich in linoleic acids (Omega-6), such as vegetable oils such as grapeseed, soybean, sunflower, and peanut oil and which we find especially in industrial products such as fried foods and confectionery products.

What do Okinawan centenarians eat?

In a study carried out by Dr. Craig Wilcox, the eating habits of the typical Okinawan elder with an ordinary American citizen were compared. It found that Americans consume ten times more food of animal origin (29% versus 3% in Okinawa) and three times more fruit (20% versus 6% in Okinawa). However, Americans consume much less fish, half vegetables (16% versus 34%), and a third of cereals (11% versus 32%). On the other hand, the inhabitants of Okinawa consume many more foods rich in Omega-3 (11% against 1%) and many more products based on soy and legumes in general (12% against 1%)

The same study showed that Okinawans get less cancer and heart disease than Americans and Japanese.

The high consumption of plant-based foods by the elderly of Okinawa favors the intake of vitamins, minerals, and phytonutrients, as well as polyphenolic compounds that stimulate the production of endogenous antioxidants that fight the action of Free Radicals which are the due to premature aging of cells and the consequent onset of various diseases such as cancer, multiple sclerosis, diabetes, rheumatoid arthritis, Parkinson's disease, Alzheimer's, etc.

THE ACTION OF HERBS AND SPICES FOR A LONG AND HEALTHY LIFE

Another food characteristic of the Okinawan people is herbs and spices.

An example is "mugwort," an almost weed plant in the area that people consume daily as an antipyretic. WHO has given the project to make the mugwort plant available to developing countries for its malaria-fighting power the highest priority.

Green tea in Okinawa is also consumed many times a day. Many researchers confirm that it is very rich in polyphenols ( epicatechins ) that appear to protect against cancer.

Another spice that never fails on Okinawan tables is turmeric.

Turmeric has one-fifth the potency of cisplatin (a chemotherapy drug). It has an anti-inflammatory power and seems to protect against tumors, promotes the production of endogenous antioxidants, helps reduce cholesterol and triglycerides, and is an excellent ally for our heart. It is also able to inhibit the production of new fat cells.

To be assimilated, turmeric needs suitable combinations such as black pepper or green tea or even with a source of fat. In the absence of one of the three elements, the bioavailability of turmeric would be almost nil.

According to recent studies, turmeric could also have a decisive action preventing Alzheimer's or senile dementia.

Five grams per day of turmeric is enough to take full advantage of its properties.

The diet of Okinawan centenarians is therefore rich in polyphenols and vitamins, thanks to the daily consumption of fruit and vegetables. It is rich in Omega-3, thanks to the consumption of algae and fish. It is rich in spices with anti-inflammatory and antioxidant action.

FOOD IS NOT ENOUGH FOR HEALTHY LONGEVITY!

Are we sure that eating positive foods is enough to achieve a healthy old age?

HARA HACHI BU is the principle on which the people of Okinawa base their diet. Means EAT UP TO 80% SATIETH. The old saying of getting up from the table with 20% hunger is applied daily.

Eating less does not necessarily mean depriving oneself of the nutrients necessary for survival. But on the contrary, it means enhancing the nutraceutical effect of every meal, gaining health and longevity.

The Okinawan meal is three to four times more voluminous and nutritious yet only contains half the calories of a burger.

For the centenarians of Okinawa, however, two other factors play a fundamental role in addition to food.

The first is the outdoors and on the go. Everyone practices gardening or cultivating the vegetable garden, and the hours spent in this activity allow them to fill up on Vitamin D.

Vitamin D deficiency accelerates heart disease and can lead to bone fragility and the weakening of muscles, thus increasing the risk of bone fractures.

The second concerns social Life and the almost total absence of stress. They enjoy the company of their peers daily while sipping sake and having some small talk and never fail to take an afternoon nap.

I REVEAL THE SECRET OF THE OKINAWA PEOPLE

Here is the secret of Okinawa, it is no longer so secret, and we can summarize by saying that five simple rules can help us improve our Life by making them longer and healthier:

Define an Ikigai: Getting up in the morning with a specific goal gives us the awareness of being needed and, therefore, the right motivation to love each other.

Follow a plant-based and low-calorie diet.

Consume foods rich in fiber, polyphenols, and Omega-3s and low in fat and salt.

Gardening or exercising every day and outdoors

Develop a stable social life.

Furthermore, the Okinawans apply another concept: yuimaru, a term that in the Okinawan dialect means "circle of reference." In summary: each individual is part of a nucleus, a community, to which an indissoluble bond of mutual aid links him. This does not deprive its members of their respective independence; instead, it encourages it. But it also underlines the importance of the willingness to help the "neighbor" in any situation and at any cost. A lesson for those who, over the years, tend to take the partner for granted, "forgetting" his pleasure, his needs, his times.

On the other hand, the " yuimaru, "underlies the concept of independence of the individual, that is, the possibility for the elderly to continue to work and be independent of their children while continuing at the same time to be still helpful to their family and the whole community.

And they still practice tai chi every day.

Okinawans respect their bodies and the nature around them.

It is a diet closely linked to the traditions of the past and of the land in which they are consumed in large quantities:

Vegetables: Yellow, orange, and green, rich in antioxidants and nutrients, are eaten raw and cooked. In particular, yellow and orange fruits and vegetables are full of carotenoids. These substances reduce inflammation, increase growth and development, and improve immune system function, which is critical in maintaining health as we age...

- Tubers: especially the purple sweet potato

- Legumes: mainly soy (tofu, miso, natto, and sauces)

- Fish and seaweed: fish is usually eaten 3-4 times a week, while the most common seaweeds are kombu, nori, and hijiki

- Green tea and jasmine tea: are the popular drinks in Okinawa

- Soy tofu

- Foods that are consumed with a lot of limitations:

Meat: Although the Okinawan diet allows for meat consumption (pork is eaten, for example), it does so in small quantities, especially during holidays or special occasions. The inhabitants generally consume a mainly vegetable diet for the rest.

Cereals: especially those with gluten, to be avoided as this protein consumed in excess can cause digestive problems, inflammation, difficulty in absorbing nutrients, and allergic reactions. Steamed brown rice and quinoa are most commonly consumed.

Dairy: Okinawans and most Asian cultures consume very little milk. When you eat milk or dairy products, you prefer raw, as pasteurization causes them to lose valuable substances. The alternatives are coconut milk or almond milk.

**Okinawan diet, how it works**

It is a relatively poor sugar and cereal diet. It has been calculated that Okinawans consume approximately 30% less sugar and 15% fewer cereals than the rest of Japan.

Then there is a fundamental concept that is found in the saying "Hara Hachi Bu, "taught by Confucius, who reminds his followers that the key to not overeating is to stop eating when you are eighty percent full. Therefore, we must get a little more appetite from the table, but not too much!

It is, therefore, essential not only what one assumes but also the fact of learning to eat consciously and slowly, focusing on what and how it is consumed (a style of eating very different therefore from the more frequent hit and run type of the West).

This strategy pays off. Okinawans typically consume about 1,200 calories a day, far fewer than the 2,000 of the mainland Japanese. Still, because the foods they put on the table are so rich in nutrients, they can stay healthy and live longer, even if on less.

**Okinawan diet, benefits**

The benefits of this diet are mainly due to the consumption of many vegetables, legumes, whole grains, fish, and algae. Even a drink like green tea affects health when consumed regularly.

Anti-age, therefore, helps to fight cellular aging thanks to the contrasting action on free radicals.

Low risk of osteoporosis: thanks to the consumption of soy and derivatives and raw vegetables, the inhabitants of Okinawa can take on good levels of calcium, whose absorption is also favored by the Isoflavonoids present in soy.

Less risk of heart problems and hypertension: thanks to the diet they follow, the Okinawans have a lower risk of dealing with high cholesterol and triglycerides, atherosclerosis, hypertension, and diabetes.

Lower cancer risk: the inhabitants of the Japanese island are less likely to get sick from certain types of cancer.

No overweight and obesity: eating well and in a reduced way means that these problems typical of Western societies are avoided.

Low oxidative stress and inflammation: calorie restriction, or the intake of fewer calories, ensures that Okinawans can always keep oxidative stress and inflammation at the root of various diseases under control.

However, all these benefits would be attributable to nutrition and, more generally, to a healthy lifestyle. In fact, in Okinawa, health and longevity are also maintained with other systems:

Practicing Tai Chi, Kobudo (local martial art), and meditation

Dedicating oneself to one's spirituality

Through a strong network of friends and family

In essence, eating well, keeping stress at bay, practicing physical activity, and having a good dose of social interaction are the secrets of the long Life of the inhabitants of the Japanese island that we, too, can treasure.

# CHAPTER 13

# THE CONCEPT OF OMOIYARI

S elflessness, empathy, sympathy, and prosocial behavior. In a word, " omoiyari "is the Japanese art of taking care of others actively and selflessly.

Even if differently, the events of recent times have touched everyone, showing the world how much unity, understanding of others, kindness, compassion, and respect are fundamental values to move forward and overcome even the most difficult situations. Hard. Concepts that can be grouped and combined under one Japanese word, " omoiyari."

A key concept at the base of Japanese culture manifests itself in every area of Japanese Life (but not only).

Trying to find the meaning of this word, one could easily (and erroneously) conclude that " omoiyari " is the equivalent of empathy and sympathy. That is the ability to understand, to put oneself in another person's shoes, situation, or state of mind.

A conscious understanding of what is happening, more on a cognitive than an emotional level. And this is precisely the substantial difference between these concepts.

**What is omoiyari?**

The Japanese term omoiyari goes further, indicating the

sensitivity of an individual to imagine and understand the feelings and what someone else is experiencing (without necessarily having experienced it firsthand) and behaving accordingly. Take care of others, try to understand who you are in front of, and do so.

The word omoiyari is made up of two distinct terms omoi and yari. The first, omoi, refers to another concept, thought towards others, their emotions or feelings, towards their thoughts, memories, or desires. A study intended to take care of all these aspects and, above all, of oneself.

It is essential to know how to take care of yourself to take care others. By becoming aware of what one is and of the environment around us.

By yari, on the other hand, we mean doing, acting, sending something to someone.

Why is it essential to discover and bring back feelings such as empathy, compassion, and selflessness? In a book that highlights the importance of embarking on a path of personal growth for one's own and common good, try to explain it to us, Erin Niimi Longhurst. In perfect omoiyari style. A way of Life that can make a difference for a more united and kind world.

Therefore, an active concept is an intuitive understanding that is not limited only to the intention of doing but also translates into concrete actions aimed at the well-being of others, which, today more than ever, we would all need.

One could almost say that it is for the omoiyari that the whole world has stopped taking care of each other against an invisible but concrete enemy. And it is again with the omoiyari. We should start again and continue with participatory and active attention toward our neighbors.

With kindness, mutual understanding, and selfless compassion for the common good. In a certain sense, everyone feels responsible for someone else's well-being.

**History and origins of Omoiyari**

The ability and willingness to "feel" the joys and sorrows of others while helping them satisfy their desires by emotionally identifying with a person or thing.

Yuimaru, another Japanese term linked in particular to the island of Okinawa, refers to the "circle of reference" and which, among others, indicates readiness for mutual help discreetly and delicately.

A way of living, welcoming others, and thinking that is "taught" and promoted as an educational model in schools, as a guiding principle and cultural value for interacting and communicating with others.

But where does this term come from? Although a particular origin cannot be attributed to this word/concept since it was part of nature, it is first authentic; recognized appearance took place around 1978.

The episode is related to Shin Kanemaru, the Japanese Defense

Agency director-general. Explaining the Japanese government's decision to help and share the expenses incurred by the American bases in Japan, the director defined it as the support given out of "sympathy".

Support that, despite the 1960 Agreement (SOFA) on the state of the US military in Japan, which was limited to the provision of "facilities and areas," became much broader by choice and will.

A concrete step (and perhaps also the only possible one) towards overcoming individuality and towards the abolition of fear, intolerance, conflicts, and xenophobia (i.e., the aversion one feels towards foreigners and all that comes from abroad), which today is more than ever essential to overcome a large number of preconceptions, hatred, and neglect of what appears different, that is not understood, or that is frightening.

**Principles and precepts**

Based on omoiyari, four fundamental points can be identified: altruism (around which others revolve), empathy, sympathy, and prosocial behavior (the propensity to help others without seeking a reward).

The meaning attributed to the concept of altruism, when speaking of omoiyari, can be divided into:

- give/give oneself and give/provide oneself with the genuine desire to do so

- empathically understand who you are in front of no ulterior motive or claim to reward

And it is on this series of principles that the other cardinal points are based.

By empathy, we mean feeling close to another person and understanding their moods, emotions, and sensations, imagining them, and making them your own. Or, more simply, the ability to put yourself in the other's shoes.

On the other hand, sympathy is about what you feel and your inclination for another person. The consideration, concern, care, or compassion that one feels, positively, for the other.

While with prosocial behavior, it refers to the propensity to act for the benefit of another individual or groups of people with voluntary actions. Never following a request or a threat but almost (and often) anticipating the needs or desires of those close to you.

**Other principles**

But not only. The term " omoi " recalls thinking and taking care, even of oneself, as seen initially. This also manifests itself in developing and improving self-knowledge, one's awareness of needs, the emotions one feels, and how one lives. Aspects that translate into other concepts at the basis of Japanese culture such as: see the beauty of little things, avoid waste, clean and organize spaces.

A way to enhance yourself and take care of yourself at 360 °. And which is then also transmitted to everything around you, things, places, and people in every behavior of daily Life.

**Examples of omoiyari**

It is no coincidence to see the Japanese in the restaurant tidy up the table where it was just eaten or even rearrange their hotel room before leaving it or respect the direction of ascent or descent of a staircase (trivial? our subways maybe not).

But also protect from the rain, with a double envelope, the purchases you have just made or create comfortable and beautiful packages to see just to give joy to those who receive them.

Eclatant (obviously for the Western world accustomed to anything else) was also the episode during the World Cup in Russia in 2018. At the end of the match, the fans of the Japanese (and Senegalese) cleaned their stands from all waste. This is an example of total respect for the place itself and the people present or who would arrive later, including the cleaners.

Small tricks to improve the lives of others. And all attitudes are inherent in the philosophy of Life and the concept of omoiyari.

A mood-based on mutual consideration and its concrete manifestation. Active and constant participation in the search for general well-being, for oneself and others, without any distinction or discrimination. And without any pretensions.

Only as an act of unconditional love capable of obscuring the self-centeredness that too often is part of one's way of Life (how often do you think "I'll come first") in favor of what happens and that the people around us experience.

For this reason, in a historical period in which fear of what we do not know seems to prevail (be it a virus or much more simply of a person other than us), understanding and approaching the concept of omoiyari becomes the only possible solution for open up to a better future.

A future in which every action taken and every decision taken or exercised is genuinely aimed at total well-being, without prejudice, limitations, or exclusions. But only with respect for the human being and the places we live.

# CHAPTER 14

# UKEIRERU, THE JAPANESE ART OF LIVING HAPPILY AND HOW TO PRACTICE IT

C an we achieve happiness? Yes, according to the Japanese philosophy of ukeireru. Such as? By learning to practice acceptance.

How can we be happy? Consciously or not, we all seek the answer to this question. According to the Japanese philosophy of ukeireru, the solution is simpler than we think and passes through acceptance.

### Ukeireru: what does it mean?

Ukeireru in Japanese means "acceptance." More precisely, one of four terms ( Ukeireru, Uketomeru, Toriireru, and Ukenagasu ) has this meaning, each with a different nuance.

Ukeireru indicates a particular type of acceptance when a mother makes her child accept something in a kind, fun way to imagine within herself.

Ukeireru means much more than self-acceptance. It means accepting our relationships in our families, at school, at work, and in our communities. It means taking others.

### The principles of Ukeireru

So what does this philosophy of acceptance consist of? Culturally, we are led to desire more and more and to look beyond the here and now. We want more money, bigger houses, faster cars, and better jobs. On the one hand, we can't help but think about the future. On the other hand, we can hardly free ourselves from nostalgia.

We are often dissatisfied, spasmodically looking for something we cannot define and, for this reason, we cannot find. And the more we want to be happy, the more that happiness we can't grasp.

How do you get out of this vicious circle? With acceptance, the ukeireru. By accepting ourselves and what surrounds us, everything that is part of our Life makes it unique, from family to friends, through work and relationships.

Warning: accepting does not mean being satisfied, nor submitting. Ukeireru is an acceptance aimed at change, not passivity: it is a conscious choice to achieve well-being by forgetting stress, anxiety, and dissatisfaction.

Yes, because once we learn to accept our surroundings, we will have time to calmly observe and notice that we are only a part of society, not even that important. As a result, we can more easily open up other points of view and understand them without reacting impulsively to a person or event we are angry about. And we won't be so stressed and frustrated.

The strength of this lifestyle - which requires constant practice - is that by focusing on accepting ourselves, others, and the events around us, we can learn to control our thoughts, emotions, and behaviors and get our points. Of strength and weakness as an integral part of our being and accepting who we are serenely and, ultimately, assuming that we have no control over everything that happens.

**How to practice Ukeireru**

How is it practiced, then the acceptance that can lead us to happiness? Saying it is easy, practicing ukeireru instead requires an effort because it requires us to abandon the mindset with which we grew up and the culture in which we are immersed to embrace peace and satisfaction in Life.

We must become aware of ourselves first and then of what surrounds us and be able to accept it. How to do it?

Calm can be found in ritualizing small gestures, such as making coffee, drinking tea, or enjoying a cocktail, and rediscovering the importance of relaxing baths and refreshing naps. Respect for oneself and others can be practiced, with a calming effect on those around us, to be able to listen more than we speak. You can rearrange your Life by minimizing the experiences and relationships that cause more stress than relief.

Still, practical ways of dealing with anger, fear, and arguments can be cultivated. In short, by practicing acceptance, it is possible to take a break from stress and situations that make us uncomfortable to take control of our Life. The first step to change is the acceptance of reality.

# CHAPTER 15

# THE UKIYO

L iving lightly by learning to enjoy every moment, without past or future, here is Ukiyo, the particular Japanese artistic (and life) technique that teaches how to float in the world, living with serenity and tranquility.

One of the primary and fascinating characteristics of art, in all its forms, is the ability to express and give shape to the most hidden and intimate sides of the human being and all that surrounds him. It catalyzes and stops the attention of the observer in a specific mood. Ukiyo is an example.

Ukiyo is an ancient oriental painting technique and a way of living, seeing, representing, and feeling the surrounding world. There is a world between the dream and the real, between the temporary and what seems everlasting, and between the elusive and the tangible.

A natural lifestyle and a way of approaching oneself and others with a more excellent disposition of mind, seeking a state of well-being, happiness, and total and lasting tranquility.

But let's see better where this art form comes from and how it has developed over time, becoming a "form of life."

**The origins of Ukiyo**

As mentioned, Ukiyo is an artistic current and precisely a printing technique ( Ukiyo-e) born in Japan, particularly in Tokyo, during the Edo period (ancient name of Tokyo), in the second half of the 17th century.

The term comes from the union of two Japanese words: uku and yo, which mean floating and the world. "Images of the floating world" were initially represented through a particular artistic print on paper with wooden matrices.

The technique became famous thanks to the development of a new bourgeois class of wealthy traders and artisans and the rising demand for a new type of art, closer to reality and less to tradition.

A reality that loved to immerse sufferings and worries in the pleasures of the world, forgetting the Buddhist teachings that defined it, in fact, as a sort of floating world.

Therefore, for the first century of production, the most represented subjects were elegant women, markets, banquets, and even erotic scenes, reflecting the life of an era in which it was easy to let pleasures take oneself. Living in that "floating world," made up of temporary goods and needs to which (according to the Buddhist tradition) one should not cling.

If initially, therefore, the Ukiyo-e began to be produced to illustrate stories and books, representing scenes of everyday life. They soon became independent productions (such as postcards or posters) thanks to their success.

## Art as synthesis and clarity

Despite this approach to life at the time, however, the government in the office always proved intolerant of any form of exaggeration. Including color in the images to limit their use to only eight colors.

It was a very restrictive imposition for painting and printing, but rather than impoverishing art, it exalted it, thanks to the genius of artists such as the masters Hokusai and Hiroshige. These, bringing to life the values of the Buddhist tradition, began to draw the essence from what was represented, enhancing nature concerning the man in a direct but always pleasant and sophisticated way.

The story in images of a specific moment, a way of living the moment, savoring every facet, without past or future time but only as a representation of the present. Simple actions from washing a horse, fishing in a river and acting in the rain to the vision of a raging wave approaching the shore.

Ukiyo as a painting technique

Images that were initially monochromatic. The artist created the first drawing on paper using only ink with this woodblock printing technique. The design was then superimposed face down on a block of wood, on which only the white parts of the paper were engraved, destroying the original design.

Once done, the woodblock was inked and printed like a rudimentary photocopier.

The prints obtained from the original were then positioned and glued face up on other wooden blocks, leaving the areas to be colored in relief. A rather complex process that requires the work of various figures, designers, carvers, printers, etc.

Therefore, the finished print came from the union of these colored blocks differently and which, repeatedly superimposed, produced the final design.

The themes that mainly were interpreted and that still today are attributable to the artistic vein of Ukiyo are:

- the theater;

- tradition, in which the protagonists are legendary characters, poets, spirits and monsters of rivers or mountains, etc .;

- the landscape, as a description of natural environments but also the typical paths of the Japanese;

- the city, the daily life, the actions and activities of the ordinary people, such as artisans, street vendors, merchants;

- nature is understood as what inhabits it. Rocks, flowers, animals. Everything is alive and has a soul, and it is precisely this that the artists represent;

- female beauty, which has always been a cornerstone of art, has witnessed its change over the centuries.

Over time this particular technique spread more and more among Japanese artists, so much so that it became the most studied and famous Japanese art form in the world.

The artists

Even today, when it comes to Japanese art, one of the greatest masters of Ukiyo-e immediately comes to mind, Katsushika Hokusai (stage name of Katsushika Sori). Creator of sketches, poems, shunga prints (images for adults), and works of art such as the series "36-Views of Mount Fuji," of which the most famous is "The Great Wave of Kanagawa. "

In addition to the great wave, Mount Fuji is represented (protagonist of the work) and some sailors at the mercy of the sea. Enclosing a deep sense of the sublime and the awareness of how small man is compared to nature.

But he is certainly not the only representative of Ukiyo. Among others also, Kitagawa Utamaro is known for his female illustrations, which greatly influenced the image of Japanese beauty worldwide and had a substantial impact on the artistic production of the European Impressionists of the 19th century.

Another Japanese artist exponent of Ukiyo, Utagawa Hiroshige, whose art impressed the painter Vincent Van Gogh so much that he replicated it in some of his works in a new and personal version.

A defined and recognizable artistic language based on living and transferring the moment as a unique and unrepeatable instant.

It is a way to capture the present moment, the here and now, learning to live it in art and real life, savoring it in all its facets. With lightness, without past or future, free from stress and everyday thoughts.

**Ukiyo as an approach to life**

Ukiyo sublimates the ability to enjoy the moment inherent in everything, a way of approaching life new, different, and capable of detaching from the frenzy of every day to discover the beauty in everything, canceling all the others for a moment. Thoughts.

A philosophy of life that pushes you to observe and fully enjoy the little one, every detail contained in all those moments of life that are often absorbed by the chaos of everyday life, getting lost.

A floating world is made up of everything ephemeral (but in a positive key), beautiful and alive, in us and around us. In a painting, in a poem, and in the concrete and real-life of each one. And this is precisely what the term Ukiyo indicates, the ability to live and enjoy the emotions of the present moment.

What derives from it is a feeling of peace, tranquility, and generalized well-being that spreads within oneself, as a state of mind, and in what one does, acting and perceiving.

Living in a fluctuating world presumes to detach oneself from the disturbances, suffering, and stress of everyday life, or rather, to let them pass without being overwhelmed by them, creating a state of essential serenity both interior and exterior.

**The benefits of Ukiyo**

Ukiyo is a natural lifestyle that applies to one's inner

predisposition and envelops and involves the way and the environment in which one lives.

From the colors used for the furniture (possibly light or that recall nature) to the choice of comfortable shapes. From dedicating moments to oneself to taking care of others to reaching a state of harmony, serenity, and total tranquility.

The same concept of welcome and intimacy can be found in two other philosophies of life, the Hygge typical of the Danish people or the Lagom, originally from Sweden. Both (albeit differently) focused on achieving personal happiness and whom you have it around.

Applying Ukiyo to one's way of being and living implies achieving a mental state of peace and pleasure. The same feeling that one would have when looking at a beautiful work of art, but which is transmitted in every aspect of one's life.

In this way, you learn to enjoy every moment, moment by moment, dedicating yourself to moments of relaxation as a sort of natural recharge that affects both physical and mental health, which is too often undermined by the frenzy of modern life.

Stress, anxiety, lack of time and self-care, bad habits, etc., all contribute to damaging one's well-being and the health of body and mind.

Practicing Ukiyo can be a concrete help to focus on the present, on the sensations and emotions that one feels and of which it is essential to take care.

**Tips for practicing Ukiyo**

Living following this philosophy means cultivating a set of both internal and external aspects. A 360 ° way of living, from furniture to taking care of yourself. All aim to search for tranquility and beauty, filling one's life with positive energy.

To do this, you can follow some small tricks that can help you immerse yourself in this new mood of life. For example, starting from what one knows, such as one's home, the place par excellence where one takes refuge and where one should feel welcomed and at peace.

Opting for neutral, light colors that recall nature (such as sand, gray, dove gray, white, etc.) is an excellent method to surround yourself with tranquility and create an atmosphere of well-being.

As well as, the presence of plants, preferably real ones, helps to induce calm and harmony. But not only that: the shape of the objects, the images (perhaps in Ukyio style ), and their arrangement can influence how spaces are lived and perceived. Together, all elements give an atmosphere and a state of mind of calm and positivity.

But not only. Dedicate moments to yourself or even just take the time to do things, without haste, without already thinking about what you will have to do next, lightly and focusing solely on the present as the only moment to live fully. From cooking to preparing a relaxing bath, enjoying the commute to work to savor the food you eat.

You live every emotion as unique and unrepeatable as is every single moment of life itself. A still image capable of arousing emotions and feelings and which, just like a work of art, is capable of making those who observe it feel good and live it, day by day.

# CHAPTER 16

# ICHIGO RICHIE

Ichigo Richie (in its original version 一 期 一 会) is a word related to Zen Buddhism and takes its origins from the tea ceremony. Its meaning could be translated as "for some time, an opportunity" and means precisely that for every moment lived, there is, for every "time," an unrepeatable opportunity that cannot be granted another of those moments.

一 期 一 会 is an awareness that has tended to touch everyone throughout their life. Being in the present moment is also a condition sought by most, if not in existence in general, in tiny fractions of freedom reserved for oneself. It could be identified in that thing that "chases" itself in the search for contact with the sea, or with nature in general, or it could be directly found in the space of silence.

It can be caught 一 期 一 会 while you are working on something that requires intellectual skills while trying to "attract inspiration" or in performing manual acts while letting go with the mind. It can come during a moment of extreme awareness of the fact that the people who are living in that moment will soon be gone while enjoying a surprise or a special gift (received or given), and on all those occasions in which one places oneself in a listening position in a broad sense.

Fortunately, there are countless moments of beauty that can be crossed by the awareness of Ichigo ichie, even without knowing its origins and "definitions," - which means welcoming the nuances of life so that they do not go unnoticed pass through us.

### The origins of the Ichigo culture ichie

Wanting to take a deep look at the Ichigo culture ichie, it is - as anticipated - a philosophy that originates from the tea ceremony. Initially, it was a man named Murata Shukō who transformed the tea tasting moment from a simple meeting between friends to a delicate moment of sharing between a few people.

After him, Sen no Rikyu, a Japanese Buddhist monk of the sixteenth century, enriched the concept of the tea ceremony, transforming it into an actual ritual and revolutionizing the structure of the respective room. In this context (as also indicated in the text " Ichigo ichie "by Héctor Garcìa and Francesc Miralles ), the word Wabi was coined precisely by Sen no Rikyu, together with Takeno Joo and Murata Juko, and the tea ceremony known as Wabi cha originated.

The Wabi cha focuses on simplicity with minimalist tools and the essentiality of the place where the ceremony takes place. What is essential is that a neutral environment is created, which prevents you from escaping into the past or the future, thus obliging you to remain concentrated in the present. Each of the five senses must be focused on what happens during the ceremony, as it is the only way to fully enjoy the moment.

From the tea ceremony, the inchigo ichie has become a universal concept, helpful in defining a higher level of attention in everyday things, and it is always simpler to understand but more delicate to implement concretely, as it is fundamental in a society that often gets used to filling moments more than to be present in them.

Capturing the essence of the moment means Ichigo ichie. Living the present moment as unique and unrepeatable makes you happier.

Living the moment consciously, putting this simple concept into practice, means having understood what Ichigo means ichie.

Practicing Ichigo ichie means giving up the habit of taking everything for granted and starting to give value to every moment of the day.

Every moment is unique and unrepeatable, yet often, taken from everyday life, we lose pieces of life that we will never find again. Ichigo ichie is a word that encourages you to live every moment as if it were your last, fully expressing emotions and feelings.

If you are with someone you love, you are sure you will never see them again, what would you do?

Would you hug her? How much time would you spend with her? How many moments do you spend with your children or parents without paying them due attention?

I decided to consciously live the Ichigo Ichie to give value to every meeting, moment, and event as if it were unique and unrepeatable.

Life is a gift. Living it and giving value to every moment is the best form of gratitude. In this article, you can read how this emotion, gratitude, improve your life.

**How to practice Ichigo ichie**

Practicing Ichigo ichie means living in the present, letting go of the past, and not worrying about the future. All we need is here and now. Living it as a gift, living it entirely, means capturing a piece of life forever.

Life is a series of unrepeatable opportunities. No one day is the same as another, let alone one instant equal to another. When we greet a person, no one guarantees us that we will see them again. Each time, let's get used to saying goodbye as if it were a once-in-a-lifetime encounter.

Let's hug our loved ones, friends, and people we care about. Let's do it at every meeting because every meeting is unique.

**How to practice Ichigo ichie**

Seize the moment with Ichigo ichie

Breaking the routine or breaking out of the daily patterns in which we have pigeonholed our life. Once in a while, let yourself go, let go of the things you usually do and indulge in something new.

When you choose to live some moments as if they were unique and special, dedicated only to you, you attract new experiences, encounters, and fluctuations. Listen to your heart, learn to trust your feelings, and move towards them.

The moment something is born inside you. As a result, the

universe sends you the exact correspondence. You may be amid a spiritual awakening. To find out, read this article.

Enjoy the present moment.

Starting to put into practice the principles of Ichigo ichie, it is natural for you to take your foot off the accelerator. Going slower, you will enjoy the beauty of the landscape. You will fully experience the moments that you did not even notice before.

Stop if you can, and let the senses convey their message to you. Perceiving reality in this way will help you appreciate the richness of life.

### The change with Ichigo ichie

Being aware of every moment of life leads us to avoid any waste of time. If what you do does not make you happy, practicing Ichigo Ichie will be natural for you to make those changes that can add value to your time.

The universe, in this regard, often sends us signals in the form of coincidences. Get into the great habit of writing every day in a notebook, events, meetings, and anything else you think can be helpful to understand the way forward.

This Japanese philosophy, which has its roots in Zen Buddhism, reminds us in vast letters of the fragility of life.

Valuing every meeting, hugging our loved ones tightly every time we leave the house and return. They seem to be taken for granted, yet, today's frenzy and excessive individualism have accustomed us to losing the true essence of human relationships.

With the Ichigo Ichie, we have the opportunity to regain possession of our time and, ultimately, of our life. Happiness depends on the rules you have given yourself. In this article, you can find out how to be happy every day.

# CHAPTER 17

# THE SHINING YOKU

The evolution of civilization, production techniques, and the expansion of cities have provided greater comfort to our life. We have work, a series of electronic devices that help us in everyday life, and we are facilitated in all our actions.

So why do we always feel terribly out of phase?

Because all the progress we are looking at so positively, on the other hand, is taking away from us something ancestral and significant: the nature that gave us life.

We live a gray life

Our alarm clock rings very early in the morning. We have a busy schedule of work commitments, appointments with friends, and domestic duties within our homes.

After a quick breakfast, we must enter the gray of our cars, enter an even darker flow of smog and distress, and then sit all day in a building that probably has few windows.

Of the exasperated urbanization of our society, we only see the climate change it is leading to, a factor which we have only been concerned about in the last few years.

But what about the change it brings about in our souls? In mind and the heart?

Perhaps you feel that this kind of life allows you external well-being but does not satisfy you entirely internally. And you don't know why.

The answer to these questions is only one: you lack nature.

Shinto, the doctrine that attributes a soul to natural elements

This particular doctrine originates in Japan. Therefore, according to shintola nature, all the plants, animals, and waters that compose it are endowed with a soul.

Indeed, the Japanese worship the oldest trees or the most special ones as real deities.

We, Westerners, have entirely lost any connection with nature. We do not worship it, but we also don't respect it.

If a tree has grown where the threads of light pass, we do not bother to cover the lines or divert their path, we simply cut down the tree. The same happens to building roads, creating arable fields, or obtaining building plots.

We take what we need from nature, the raw materials we need to produce all the material objects that are part of our life, and we do not worry that the heart is also composed of living beings.

We feel almost dissociated as if we live in a world and she is in a parallel dimension. This is demonstrated by this great fact that we get nervous when animals or insects enter the house. We consider that aseptic environment, while we were born in the middle of nature.

Shinrin was born in Japan, this distant and poetic land where each element fulfills a particular function.

**Shinrin yoku, the bathroom in the forest**

For the Japanese, shinrin yoku can be translated as "bathroom in the forest." It is a natural philosophy that encourages individuals to frequent the forests more, get in touch with the nature they are losing, and nourish their spirit with positive sensations.

The Japanese forestry authority introduced this concept in the early 1980s. With this novelty, we wanted to induce the inhabitants of large cities such as Tokyo, Kyoto, and Osaka to seek that contact with nature that they were losing.

There is an ancient belief that the forest has a healing power on the body and mind.

To confirm this theory was also the well-known journal "Science," which has scientifically demonstrated the beneficial power of nature on health. The study took a sample of patients who had just had a cholecystectomy. Those who had the window of the room overlooking nature were shown to be more positive, react better to treatment, and arrive faster to recovery.

**We are nature: apply shinrin yoku**

All living forms were born thanks to nature and belong to it; the same thing also applies to man. He may decide to live in concrete buildings, move with sheet metal casings, and walk with his feet well protected by shoes. But we cannot deny our origins.

110

We are one with nature.

iWhen we feel out of phase and unbalanced; we can simply take refuge inside it. There is no need for extensive forests, just a garden or a public park.

An exercise you can do to relax your mind is to go to a forest and start touching the plants. Run a hand over the bark, listen to the vital lymph flowing and surrender to this feeling of peace.

You can also sit by the tree or lie down. The main thing is to maintain close contact with the vegetation.

We are aware of this approx change when we travel. While living in the countryside, we too have lost direct contact with nature.

When we are traveling, we spend hours admiring the ocean crashing on the beach, we walk in silence in the woods watching how the light creeps between the canopies of the trees, and we are outdoors as much as we can.

The next time you have a free moment during the day, don't put yourself in front of the TV, but go out for a walk and reconnect your soul to nature by being inspired by shinrin yoku.

Scientific research in recent years has produced numerous studies aimed at demonstrating the profound well-being generated by the recovery of our connection with nature (many of them focus on the world of children), thus corroborating our innate orientation towards "biophilia," a term already used by Aristotle, recovered by Fromm and forcefully returned to the fore in more recent times. Biophilia (from the Greek: phillia, friendship, love and bios, life) is the natural propensity of human beings to generate bonds of friendship and affiliation with other living beings. It is an innate attitude developed through millions of years of evolution about nature and other forms of life: organisms, species, and habitats. Cooperation (not competition) between different species is the heart of ecosystems, where difference is a competitive advantage, inter-species collaboration a resource, and multi-sensory engagement in experience is necessary for survival.

This concept also exists in Western culture.

Today neuroscience shows us that brain patterning (i.e., the construction of new neuronal paths and brain patterns, which give life to actions, attitudes, thoughts, and behaviors) is based on sensory inputs. So: the more significant the richness of our sensory experience, the greater our patterns of thought and action, and the better we can manage in life. However, the strong diffusion of electronic media goes in the opposite direction to enriching the sensory experience, loading the sense of sight and progressively atrophying the other four senses available to human beings.

In addition to this progressive dispossession of sensoriality, the screens we use more and more every day (monitors, smartphones, tablets, etc.) emit high-energy light radiations (blue-violet rays), which in addition to favoring the gradual decline of visual function, modify our ability to produce melatonin (the hormone regulating the sleep-wake cycle), interfering with our ability to rest at night, and generating hyperactivity and lack of concentration in children.

On the other hand, studies show how much outdoor activities and deep connection practices in nature restore our living system to its full vital and creative potential and are increasingly used in the therapeutic, rehabilitative, educational, and training fields as strategies. Essential in recovering our connection with ourselves and consequently with our well-being. Nature activates our natural ability to feel good in the world, in the world, and with the world.

Another exciting line of research concerns the impact of recovering a sense of closeness and relationship with the natural environment and other living beings on the ecological behavior of people. In comparison, those who continuously cultivate their relationship with the natural world manifest greater ecological awareness and the desire to commit to protecting the environment and living species proactively.

Those who live in nature inevitably learn to love it and defend it in case of a threat. Today, ecology must start from regaining our relationship of affiliation and affection with the natural world, with the earth that is our mother, because it forged our living system over millions of years of evolution. In this regard, Jon Young (the founder of the international movement of the Deep Connection with nature,) however, points out that it is not so much the amount of time we spend in nature that makes the difference, but the way we are in essence, what we do, the quality of the attention we devote to experiencing nature, and not just "in nature." It is one thing to do outdoor activities. Another is to recover the living sense of our connection with the natural world: this requires a different quality of attention and presence, which can be developed over time and with practice, as we would with any other discipline...

This is what the awakening practices of our primitive intelligence services, and here I propose a taste of it, to be done immediately, in the green remnant that is most convenient and close to you: the experience always begins where you are. It is unnecessary to look for the three-thousand-year-old redwoods on the other side of the world to have a "real" experience. Even the tree in the parking lot below the house can be for you (and will tell you about your nature as a man or woman of the city, much more than a sequoia in an uncontaminated park!).

**Sensory walk**

Devote at least 20 'to this simple practice that you can do while walking in an open place. Suppose you are in a park or nature. In that case, you can take advantage of a relaxing acoustic environment for your deep psyche (birdsong has a calming effect on our archaic brain, which is used to associate it with the absence of dangers). If you are in a city or on the street with a lot of urban traffic, switching off the thought will be more difficult. listen from inside your feet, and listen to the ground beneath you from inside your feet, for a few moments, sinking your attention into the rhythmic alternation of feet on the basis as they walk. From there, gradually bring your attention to your whole body, segment by segment: listen to the ankles, the knees, the entire legs, the hips and pelvis, the belly, the back, the chest, the space of the heart, the vertebral shaft in its undulatory movement, then up towards the shoulders and arms, up to the heart of the hands. Then go up with attention to the nape, the root of the head, the skull, and everything inside. Finally, the face: listen to your expression, eyes, and ears from within. And in this review of your entire living system, make sure that your walk is transformed into a self-massage, and each step allows you to loosen the joints, making you more and more fluid with each step. Let the breath melt everything. Let yourself breathe everywhere, from the feet to the head. Let your walk be a walk that lives smoothly, from foot to head, as much as possible without blockages and contractures.

**A walk is a massage: a walk that is a pleasure, one step after another.**

When you have thus reconstructed your perception of yourself (usually the minimum time you will need will be at least 10 '), leave a little attention on the walk-self-massage, and bring the rest of your attention to the environment around you.

And open your senses, one after the other, about what surrounds you.

First, listen to the sounds around you, from the farthest to the closest, at 360 °. Focus them all, one by one. And finally, embrace all the sounds in a single awareness, grasp the reciprocal relationships, the resonances, the counterpoints, and how the sounds integrate and dance with each other in a single orchestra. Then bring your attention to what your sense of smell perceives, your taste, and finally, the tactile sensations that reach your skin: the air that touches the uncovered skin, the effect of the sun, the caress of a leaf as you pass underneath. a tree…

Finally, synaesthetically embrace in single attention all the sensory inputs that you have mapped, putting together your sensations of yourself as you walk, from the feet to the head, all whole in the breath, with the feelings that come from your surroundings. And stay as long as you like in this conscious walking, as long as it is good for you, as long as you want.

You can repeat the experience described below in different contexts and observe the response of your system to the different environments you will go to—an exciting experiment to help you listen to where you feel most at ease and feel greater well-being. And to choose where to spend more time accordingly.

Practicing alone is essential, but practicing in a group makes everything much easier and faster. The group is a great resource activator. We invite you to practice conscious walking and many other practices of connection with nature together on the starting path of "Nature Connection." To discover many simple and natural methods, which can also be done alone, to rediscover the pleasure of feeling good in the world, in the world, with the world, thanks to the regenerating power of the natural world.

# CHAPTER 18

# MEDITATION

I t is a fact: proven by millennia of studies in favor and scientific research, we are now aware that meditating is suitable for physical and psychological health. Whether we search online or browse pages and pages of books, we will never find a single source that claims that meditation does harm.

There are so many different practices… so different that some types of meditation practically say the opposite of others. Even scientific studies on meditation are not divided equally for each meditation practice. Still, the most studied of all, the one for which the scientific results are most proven, is mindfulness meditation.

How to start approaching the world of meditation?

We will explore the most popular meditation techniques, starting from Buddhism to ending with the Christian one, without forgetting to highlight the practices with more scientific studies behind them.

But first … first, let's try to understand how to meditate.

**Focus or Monitoring**

First, it is good to distinguish meditation into two main strands: focus and monitoring.

This distinction is not clear-cut since, in meditation practice, focus and monitoring are intertwined.

## Focus

In a meditation that belongs to the focus of your attention, your focus is directed towards a particular "something."

One can focus on the breath, a mantra, an image, the part of the body, etc.

Don't worry, it's normal. Achieving the ability to maintain a high flow of attention to the chosen thing is complicated and becomes stronger as the practitioner advances. Over time, you will get distracted less easily. You will develop a depth and strong attention that allows you to absorb and perceive all the beneficial properties of the sweet art of meditation.

## Monitoring

Instead, the meditations that belong to the monitoring trend suggest focusing attention on observing one's thoughts in a non-judgmental way.

Mind you. This doesn't mean getting lost in your thoughts.

We must not identify with the thoughts but let them flow without judging them...

The meditation techniques that have developed over the centuries are truly innumerable.

Each geographical area, tradition, philosophy, and current of thought has developed its methods (often very different from each other) to immerse oneself in meditation. While this variety of techniques ensures that each of us can find the one that best suits our personality, on the other hand, newbies are often confused and disoriented when it comes to learning to meditate.

Therefore, the question that all beginners ask themselves is always the same: which meditation technique is right for me?

We have prepared this mini-guide specifically to clarify this doubt and provide the undecided with a general idea of the most common types of meditation, their main characteristics, and their origins. We hope it can help you orient yourself among the tangle of existing reflections and provide you with initial support to find the one best suits your personality and goals.

### Zen Meditation ( Zazen )

Zen or Zazen meditation is the classic Buddhist sitting meditation with which we all associate the concept of meditation. In the sixth century AD, it was conceived by an Indian monk and is practiced while sitting cross-legged. The breath and the stillness represent the fulcrum of this meditation: it is necessary to focus to always remain in the present with the mind.

Its benefits are increased awareness, observation skills, and self-control.

### Transcendental Meditation

Transcendental meditation is a meditation technique practiced through the recitation of a mantra. It was devised by the Maharishi master Mahesh Yogi in India in 1955 and introduced to the West in the late 1960s.

To practice it, we need to find the most suitable mantra and recite it with our eyes closed for a certain time every day.

Its benefits are a renewed harmony with our being and the whole world around us and a sense of tranquility and inner peace develops.

### Vipassana meditation

Vipassana derives from "vision," Its origins date back to the sixth century BC. It is practiced by focusing all the attention on an object, material or immaterial, and its movements.

It allows us to elevate our spirituality to a higher stage, from which a new, much more enlightened vision of life derives.

### Mindfulness Meditation

Mindfulness is a branch of vipassana meditation, developed around the 1970s for "westernizing" its concepts. Mindfulness is based on three key concepts: observing and not judging, the here and now (focusing on the present), and emotional transparency (analyzing our actions without preconceptions).

Its benefits are the cancellation of pain through awareness and total acceptance of ourselves.

### Ho'oponopono

The name identifies a Hawaiian healing method with very ancient origins, which has turned into a type of meditation over time. Similar to transcendental meditation, it is practiced by reciting a mantra (which in this case is only one). It is used to heal inner wounds, practice the art of forgiveness and find harmony with one's soul.

### Walking meditation

Walking meditation was devised by Buddha himself during his forty years of awakening while walking barefoot through the various regions of India. This meditation, as the name suggests, is practiced while walking. It lets us clear our minds of extra thoughts during the body's physical movement, helping us arrive at our destination with a much clearer mind than the starting point.

### Kundalini meditation

It is a very complex meditation technique, the ultimate goal of awakening kundalini energy, a form of energy coiled around the start of our spine.

Kundalini energy, we get full self-realization and a profound joy that flows from within our being.

### Dynamic Meditation

Dynamic meditation is part of the active meditation techniques devised by the master Osho and is the type of meditation that requires more movement and expression: it is practiced by letting our emotions and our body run free, dancing, and expressing our thoughts with irreverence. The ultimate goal is to take advantage of movement and frenzy to best channel the sensations that pervade us. As a side effect, it also allows you to appreciate silence and calm better.

Although there are many meditation techniques (and constantly expanding), you can begin to experiment with those listed here, the most widespread and widely practiced worldwide.

All you have to do is delve into the one that interests you most and whet your curiosity. Our advice is to practice each of these techniques for a week and, in the end, evaluate which one helped you focus the most and which one you found most in line with your attitudes and personality.

# CHAPTER 19

# THE TAI CHI

T ai Chi Chuan or Taiji or Tai Chi, literally the supreme art of combat, is the Chinese martial art of self-defense, which has become a training method that aims at psycho-physical well-being and helps keep the body healthy. In addition to facilitating muscle elasticity and promoting correct posture, it contributes to strengthening character.

The fundamental principle behind Tai Chi Chuan is that the body's movement should never hinder the state of inner calm. What happens around and in the practitioner's mind must not influence his state of mind: the level of balance between transparency and deep relaxation that can be reached through the practice of Tai Chi Chuan, therefore, involves both the psychic and the psychic sphere. Physics. The movements, that is, the dynamic forms, as in many martial arts, are slow and tend to follow the respiratory rhythm, as happens in the practice of vinyasa yoga, dynamic yoga.

Let's find out in detail what Tai Chi Chuan is and what benefits it can bring to the health of those who practice it regularly.

Tai Chi Chuan is a martial art suitable for everyone, old and young. The interaction between strength and flexibility characterizes it. It can invigorate the body, strengthening the immune system, so much so that it is practiced in China as an activity that promotes longevity.

It is an ancient discipline that has its roots in the Taoist tradition and the culture of Chinese martial arts; its history is linked to many schools, which have been able to spread it all over the world.

Its practice consists of repeating the sequence of slow and harmonic movements to free the mind during the course.

Five main styles follow similar principles despite having different characteristics.

- Chen

- Yang

- Wu or Hao

- Wu

- Sun

Although the different schools of Tai Chi Chuan differ from each other in their techniques, they all provide the same benefits: from stimulating the cardio-circulatory system gently to strengthening the immune system to control stress and breathing.

THE BENEFITS OF TAI CHI CHUAN: WELLNESS, STRENGTH, AND INNER CALM

Thanks to the forms, or the sequences of movements implemented during the practice, Tai Chi Chuan allows you to develop and control vital energy. With regular exercise, what is acquired is the ability not to force any movement and to perfect flexibility, smoothness of motion, and excellent muscle strength.

Therefore, well-being, endurance, and inner calm are the most evident advantages of the supreme art of fighting, but not the only ones.

Among the significant psycho-physical benefits brought by the practice of Tai Chi Chuan, we find, in fact:

• harmony between inside and outside, between mind and body;

• acquisition of adaptation as opposed to confrontation;

• awareness of time: those who practice Tai Chi Chuan soon understand that everything has a time, and the time available is sufficient to achieve in the best way what needs to be done;

• total perception of one's body, thanks to the practice of dynamic forms;

• high level of relaxation, which affects everyday life;

• training without cardiovascular fatigue;

• development of strength in the limbs and physiotherapeutic properties;

• development of balance and motor coordination;

• muscle and joint relaxation ;

• strengthening the internal organs and intestinal improvement;

- balance and abandonment of stress;

- progress of pathological states related to fibromyalgia.

## TAI CHI CHUAN, THERAPY AGAINST FIBROMIALGIA

Brown University School of Public Health, Tufts University School of Medicine in Boston, and the Center for Mind-Body Therapies in Boston found a positive correlation between fibromyalgia and a Tai Chi mind-body treatment.

The research involved 226 fibromyalgia patients in various American treatment centers: half of them underwent an aerobic exercise program for 24 weeks; the remaining half instead followed therapeutic activities based on Tai Chi Chuan, which proved to be more effective than traditional gymnastics, considerably improving the psychological and physical state of the patients.

The result reveals that the duration also affects the effects of the treatment: among the subjects involved in the practice of Tai Chi, some followed for 12 weeks, others instead of 24 weeks: well, the latter found more significant benefits.

Thai Chi could therefore prove to be an ally in the fight against this musculoskeletal syndrome whose causes are still unknown, even if, it must be said, the outcome of the study shows that this application has many limitations. The treatment was not effective in the same way for all the subjects involved; however, since it is a harmless and very light practice, it is worth evaluating it as a therapeutic option.

## The benefits of Tai Chi for over 50s: what the studies say

Among the many types of research that show the benefits of tai chi, we report two, two in particular highlight the positive effects for those who have reached middle age: one, carried out by the Shanghai University of Medicine and Health Sciences, and a study by the Department of Physical Therapy and Graduate Institute of Rehabilitation Science, College of Medicine, Chang Gung University, Taoyuan of Taiwan. Both reveal how Tai Chi Chuan, in combination with resistance training, improves physical function and muscle strength in adults aged 50 and over.

Also, according to these sources, moreover, a Tai Chi training program, modified through virtual reality, would have a protective effect on some cognitive and physical functions in the elderly with cognitive impairment. The more engaging the program, the more significant the improvement in cognitive performance.

Hence, a practice like that of Tai Chi Chuan allows us to face the everyday stressful situations that daily life subjects each of us.

Suppose it is true that Tai Chi Chuan uses dynamic forms to give mobility and flexibility to the body and mental relaxation. In such case, it is valid that we must never underestimate the possibility of a traumatic event during practice, a risk we run, in general, in any type of sporting activity. This is why it is always an excellent choice to protect yourself with a Physiotherapy Policy, which certainly does not eliminate the possibility of accidents but helps us alleviate worries (including economic ones) in case of unforeseen events.

Why not find out more?

It has very ancient origins, and its country of origin is China. Since it is a complex system of movements that moves from one position to another with fluid harmony, it is almost impossible to learn it from just a book.

It is a form of exercise/meditation that can only be passed down from one person to another.

Tai - Chi serves to achieve greater flexibility, loosens ligaments, increases the elasticity of the spine, and improves muscle tone. It also exercises a beneficial massage on the internal organs of the body.

The principle is simple. We try to make slow and agile gestures to obtain significant benefits for the body and mind. Originally it was a friar who, while observing a quarrel between a bird and a snake, imagined this technique brought back to man to achieve greater awareness of his own body.

iThey must be continuous movements to avoid jolts and abrupt stops. Combining distinct movements can involve up to 100 different activities.

Breathing is also essential in the execution. It has to be slow and deep.

Contrary to what it seems, the movements are not random. They are codified, and the chaining of gestures is part of the teaching. There are several Tai -chi- chuan schools that offer distinct specialties.

Overall, although the movements vary, the basic rules are the same:

- Raise your head

- Drop your shoulders

- Don't use force

- Always be relaxed

- Keep your joints flexible

- Making agile movements

- Do the chaining of actions continuously.

The chaining of the movements will simultaneously develop flexibility, coordination, and dynamism. In addition, breathing techniques and agile exercises allow for deep relaxation.

Tai Chi Chuan is a proven way to manage stress and find peace of mind. However, it is most effective when practiced outdoors.

Tai Chi Chuan is known as a vital health and longevity discipline. It is used a lot as a therapy in Chinese hospitals. The theory is based on its "Who" benefits. In this way, Tai -chi- chuan facilitates the circulation of the body's energy in the organism.

According to these precepts, you can get sick when the "Chi" is blocked at a specific point. This activity, therefore, also plays a preventive role against any illnesses.

During Tai -Chi, like yoga, the mind must always remain awake and aware of every movement made.

One of the primary positions is called "equestrian." Here's what it consists of:

1) Stand quietly, paying attention to each aspect of your position;

2) Still maintaining the erect position, spread the legs until the feet are perpendicular to the shoulders and parallel. This position offers a solid base of support and can also be maintained for a long time. It serves to "open" the area of the thighs and hips;

3) Keep the body straight, and the knees slightly bent forward, a little beyond the feet. This serves to lower and straighten the spine;

4) thoroughly relax the abdominal area and relax the T'an T' ien . This is the area below the navel for the Chinese, representing the body's center. In this area, the vital processes of the organism take place: digestion, sexual energy, for women, the origin of a new life;

5) Push the spine down at the base, and keep it supported in the upper area;

6) Lower the shoulders, keeping the arms away from the body, with the elbows lose and the palms facing backward;

7) Keep your head down, your mouth closed, and your eyes down;

8) You must feel grounded down and light from the waist up. By practicing this and other exercises regularly, you will soon discover that the body will adapt to various positions, which will become

natural and fluid.

Tree Root Exercise

If you feel comfortable in the "equestrian position," put your body weight on the right leg and exhale deeply.

Never forget to breathe deeply while performing the exercises. Inhale for a long time, and pay attention to feel the Qi (energy) flowing up through the right leg as you rise from the flexion, and when it reaches the right side, it will pass through the T'an T' ien (lower abdomen).

Exhale as the Qi flows through the left side. Finish with the weight fully loaded on the left leg. Keep repeating the Tai -Chi exercise until you feel in unison with the entry and delivery of your breath.

**Animals in Tai Chi Chuan**

The Taoist exercises are almost all inspired by careful observation of the movements of animals, in particular the monkey, bear, tiger, deer, and crane.

The bonds with these animals are physical, mental, and spiritual. Each animal has symbolic importance, and each has a unique quality associated with it.

**What to wear during practice**

It is best to dress comfortably and light, preferably in natural fibres (such as cotton or lightweight wool). You can move freely in a pair of sweatpants and an oversized t-shirt

You can practice Tai Chi Chuan outdoors (by the sea or in the countryside, in a park) in summer and barefoot. In winter, instead, wear a pair of light shoes with rubber soles, such as Chinese slippers.

# CHAPTER 20

# YOGA

The truth is that doing yoga at home is critically important to improving your practice, and if you don't start practicing daily, it will take you much longer to see good results.

Going to class weekly is very important to understand how to do the asanas correctly, build sequences, and know which mistakes to avoid not to get hurt. Still, it is even more important to start practicing at home too.

When I started doing yoga, to tell you the truth, I never thought you ended up opening the mat every day. Initially, you are afraid of getting hurt, of performing the positions incorrectly, you do not know what kind of sequence to practice, so you end up not doing it.

In truth, they are just excuses that the mind gives us. Over time, however, we need to overcome these small fears, doubts, and insecurities and find a way to start.

Here are the main reasons and benefits why you should do this:

1. To get to know each other better

2. To help yourself

For example, I started doing yoga for back pain, but others began with various problems. Whatever your reason, if you limit yourself to only doing yoga in class from time to time, it will take you a lot longer to feel better.

Practicing yoga at home is a real help you are giving yourself daily to improve your life and experience the profound benefits of yoga.

3. To see more improvements and in less time

Practicing at home daily allows your body and mind to get used to everything you do much faster—the new yoga positions, the recent efforts, and the new difficulties you face.

When you practice every day, the effects of each session do not even have time to disappear, and therefore the improvements are incredible.

It is essential to start doing yoga at home and necessary to do it correctly. Otherwise, you risk getting into the habit of doing a wrong practice and continuing to make the same mistakes for too long.

Buy a professional mat.

The mat is the first thing to buy when starting yoga. I say this because if you don't have one, it will happen that:

you will have to use one that is in the studio, and often the ones that are made available for new practitioners are not the best;

also, if you don't have one, you won't be able to practice at home but only in class, and this is certainly not the best way to start;

a final aspect to consider is that if the mat is not of good quality, indeed, as soon as you start sweating, you will begin to slip, and this not only does not allow you to practice at your best, but you could also get hurt. Better to avoid, right?

Attend some classes

Only a teacher can correct you, point out if you make mistakes in alignments, advise you on the best asanas if you have a specific problem, show you how not to get hurt, and use the supports to adjust the positions.

If you start entirely self-taught, it could happen that you don't know that you are making inevitable mistakes, and therefore you continue to make them for a long time. Better to avoid it, right?

My advice is to go to class at least a couple of times a week to lay the foundations for proper practice and otherwise practice at home.

Choose the type of yoga which is right for you.

The types of yoga that can now be practiced are many, and when you start, you are confused about which one to choose. There are all kinds of them, from the more static to the more lively, from the more meditative to the more physical, and from the more modern to the more traditional.

Choosing the right one, depending on how you are made and what kind of life you are leading, is very important because only in this way will you experience more significant benefits from the practice.

On the contrary, if you are practicing a style that is too slow for you or too dynamic, you can end up giving up the practice, and if you do it only because you have not found the right style, it is a great pity.

My advice is to try more than one until you feel that practice is good.

Learn more about the practice of using books as well

In my opinion, every practitioner should accompany his daily routine with the constant reading of books on yoga that allow him to deepen and improve what you are already doing. There are books on a pattern, philosophy, breathing, for beginners, for the more experienced, nutrition, anatomy, and therapeutic texts. In short, you are spoiled for choice.

Thanks to these books, I have learned a lot, and they have allowed me to improve my practice significantly at home.

If you have recently started yoga, when you begin your practice at home, you will realize that it is not that easy, and you will undoubtedly feel slightly disoriented. But don't worry, it is something you are doing for the first time and, as with all new things, it is normal for it to take some time to get used to it.

Follow the tips below.

Start gradually. There is absolutely no point in starting the practice by doing two hours every day. The body is not used to it, and neither is the mind. In this way, you will excessively exceed your limits at that moment, and it is not good. You may feel exhausted or even worse. You may get injured.

Remember that:

"If today's practice damages tomorrow's practice, it is a wrong practice."

BKS IYENGAR

So my advice is to start moderately, perhaps with 20 minutes a day, and then gradually increase both the duration of the practice and the difficulty of the positions over time.

Choose the correct type of practice.

Listen to your body, and you will identify what it needs at that moment. Because only by listening carefully to the signals it sends you can you do a practice that allows you to feel better?

Here are some examples of adapting the practice according to your situation.

If you do a job where you stay all day in yoga-backache- sitting positions, you could do a practice consisting mainly of standing yoga positions to strengthen the legs;

On the contrary, if you walk all day at work, you could mainly do positions on the ground and asanas that allow you to relax the body and legs;

If you have back pain, you may want to practice to make the pain affecting the spine go away.

If you practice in the morning, you could do a more refreshing type of practice, but a more relaxing approach is better if you practice in the evening.

If you have neck pain, you could do yoga to relax the entire neck area.

Of course, it takes some time to learn to listen to the body and modify the practice according to different situations, but everything will come with time.

Be realistic

Another aspect to consider is to be realistic with yourself.

I am realistic means considering many factors such as age, tiredness at that moment, one's flexibility, the time available, etc.

Same, if you're not too flexible, it doesn't matter. Yoga is not about being flexible. Try to overcome your limitations, but don't try to do asanas that require extreme flexibility. Otherwise, you will only get hurt.

"I would like people to realize that yoga is not touching the toes."

GARY KRAFTSOW

Add practice to your daily schedule.

To make yoga significantly improve your life, the first thing to do is to do it daily. So try to add it to the many items you have to do every day. Especially the first few times you practice yoga should be a "commitment" to be carried out with sacrifice.

I specified " especially the first few times" because the greatest sacrifice occurs the first time you do the exercises. Once you begin to experience the many benefits, giving up other less essential things is much easier to make yoga have more space.

Find your own sacred space.

Another advice I can give you to make yoga at home an excellent routine is to find your own "sacred space" to enter every time you practice.

This sacred space could be a small room, garage, garden, or just your playmat.

It doesn't matter how big it is and where it is.

The important thing is that when you enter it, you leave everything that does not concern the practice of yoga out of this space. Leave your cell phone out, your daily problems, haste, ego, and worries.

"The only thing you need to do yoga is your body and mind."

RODNEY YEE

Whenever you enter your sacred space, recite a mantra or chant, Om, and start practicing.

# CHAPTER 21

# MINDFULNESS EXERCISES TO APPLY EVERY DAY

The term mindfulness represents the concept of mindfulness, or the ability to know how to live the present moment with awareness and in a non-judgmental way.

Our mind is in constant motion: like a monkey jumping from branch to branch, it leaps from one thought to another, constantly turning to the past or the future, rarely still and aware of the present moment.

The rhythms and lifestyle of Western society do nothing but sharpen mental activity, subjecting our mind to continuous stimuli and inputs that lead us to run, organize, and think about what we should do "next."

But at "now," when do we think about it?

The mindfulness exercises that I am about to propose to you will help you to free your mind from constant external stimuli, from the whirlwind of thoughts about the past or the future, and to focus with awareness and intention in the present moment, in the famous "here and now."

### Why Practice Mindfulness?

We can train our mind to live the present consciously, without judging the thoughts that inevitably - especially at the beginning - will come, letting them go as they came, thanks to simple mindfulness exercises that help our mind to remain still and not wander.

Mindfulness helps us, first of all, to fully enjoy our time without risking it slipping through our fingers without us realizing it.

Practicing mindfulness brings benefits both psychologically and physically:

- reduces stress and anxiety

- reduces rumination, or compulsive brooding on negative thoughts and worries

- improves the ability to react to external events in a positive way

- enhances the ability to concentrate and short-term memory

- improves the immune system (yes, a positive psychological state is also reflected on a physical level ... men's Sana in corpore Sano, but also vice versa, I would say)

**How to practice mindfulness in daily life**

You don't need to abandon your daily commitments or even retreat to the Himalayas to practice mindfulness.

As already mentioned, the mind must be "trained" to live in the awareness of the present. If we start with the idea of meditating for thirty minutes from the first day, we will most likely come out discouraged and convinced that we are "not inclined" for this activity.

To start, I recommend some straightforward mindfulness exercises that will only take you 5 minutes but which, if practiced consistently, can be revolutionary.

### The cup of coffee

How often do we prepare a coffee to take a break, sit down with the cup in hand... and automatically take the phone in hand. A notification on social media, an email to check, a voice to listen to... and without us realizing it, the cup is empty, the coffee is finished, and with it also our moment of pause ?!

Try this exercise: make yourself a coffee, choose your cup carefully, and watch the hot coffee fill it as you pour it. Sit in your favorite chair, away from the phone or other distractions.

Breathe in the scent of coffee, and savor it slowly. Remain a few more minutes in silence, with your mind free of thoughts.

Then a smile, a deep breath, and consciously return to our everyday activities.

### Mandarin

Have you ever put 2 or 3 mandarins on the table and arrived at the last clove without realizing that you have eaten them?

Try this mindfulness exercise: take a tangerine, and peel it slowly. Divide one clove at a time, look at the first, smell them, and bring them to your mouth. Savor them with awareness.

For a few minutes, just focus on the mandarin you are eating. Let go of the thoughts and bring them back to Mandarin if the mind wanders.

**Five breaths**

Set an alarm clock at a chosen time of your day.

When it rings, quit the job you are doing.

Take five deep breaths. Feel the airthrough the nose and out of your mouth. Concentrate on your breaths if you can stretch them.

Count them one by one

Imagine the air you breathe expanding into your body as a new and radiant light, something fresh coming within you.

The air you exhale, identify it with all that you would like to eliminate and which you are now letting go of.

You can also set multiple alarm clocks and repeat the exercise as many times as you like throughout the day.

**The soles of the feet.**

Lie down on the bed or a mat barefoot. Put your feet together so that the soles touch. Drop your knees outward.

Notice how rarely the soles of your feet meet each other.

Remain still like this for at least five minutes, breathing consciously, feeling the soles of your feet resting and rubbing against each other.

**Tidy up the room**

Choose a room in your home to tidy up and get to work.

You will have happened to carry out this activity in a hurry, simply having the goal of having a tidy room. However, you will not be living in the present in this way. This time, just focus on the act of tidying up, completely immersing yourself in this work. Observe how the mind is present in selecting objects, making space, and cleaning drawers and surfaces. Enjoy the process. Tidying up is a cathartic activity.

These first five mindfulness exercises are ideal for those starting to approach the world of meditation.

When practiced with the right mindfulness, they are mighty and help prepare your mind for more intense meditation practices.

# CHAPTER 22

# THE MANDALAS

The Mandala is a circular structure where all points tend towards the center. Scientists would call it a rotationally symmetrical structure. The oriental vision starts from the assumption that the Mandala was created from the center, which contains everything. One might imagine that a mandala is born by blowing into a point that is thus filled with space and time. Buddhists and Hindus built and built the foundations of their temples in his image and similarly described the course of life.

In its classical form, the Mandala was represented by four towers corresponding to the four cardinal points with a symbol of unity in the middle. This indicates that several paths lead to a goal. The journey leads from the center towards the center: from the unconsciously perceived center to the center sought with awareness.

It is like in fairy tales where the protagonist starts from a point (usually his home). During his journey, he faces the world and its difficulties, makes mistakes, experiences and tests himself, discovers his resources and talents, and then goes back to the home's starting point but more mature and aware.

The Mandala is a kind of inner map that guides those who want to travel a path of personal growth. A way to bring out, welcome, and translate emotions, sensations, ideas, and experiences into color, to build or reconstruct one's internal order. It is a process that helps us move from disorder to a dynamic and new order by making our internal chaos visible and giving it shape.

The shape of the circle and the symmetry of the Mandala generates within us a perception of order and harmony: it is a defined shape that acts as a container for disjointed and confused emotions or thoughts to pass to a harmonic order. Every time we dedicate ourselves to a mandala, making silence and emptiness around us, we can listen to our innermost thoughts, to the deepest and most hidden emotions in our soul.

Making a Mandala is a void of speech because we are silent, an opening of rational thought, because whoever colors is only in contact with his soul, listening to what emerges. It is also a void of logical sense because the coloring is done simply, without any explanation. We give birth to our entire interior on the empty sheet: thus, we practice awareness!

Coloring a mandala allows us to establish a fixed point in the day and perhaps the following ones. Our soul can anchor and enable us to dedicate, with regularity and continuity, a time and a space only to ourselves, totally free from any commitment. With practice, we train ourselves to welcome, without judging it, everything that emerges from the depths.

Coloring a mandala becomes a practical mental training that promotes the mind's clarity, concentration, and tranquility. Coloring a mandala is an activity full of potential for both children and adults that should be experienced at home and school, allowing the child to experience balance, tranquility, and concentration.

In this way, it is not only a tool but can teach us the correct mental attitude with which to face life.

**How to create, draw or color a Mandala**

There are several ways to create, draw or color a mandala.

You can use shells, leaves, pebbles, flower petals, and colored earth and draw it on the sand, snow, and the water.

Or create it and color it with markers, pastels, watercolors, and tempera. Usually, it is erased or burned, and in this way, the Mandala also teaches us to practice non-attachment.

The Mandala, in all its forms, allows us to:

1- learn to manage borders, to accept the fundamental ones, but also to freely structure the space in between;

2-find oneself, calm down, and renew one's strength;

3-center and concentrate while remaining relaxed

4-orient yourself towards a model of life;

5-better integrated experiences;

6-learn to live in resonance with a model;

7-live experiences of unity;

8-develop a harmonious personality

9- draw strength from one's center.

And in this way, the Mandala offers our soul precious visual paths that illuminate our journey through life: from the center and towards the center.

The colors give emotional depth to the experience by acting on a physical and spiritual level.

Color acts on a vibrational level ( Luscher ), evoking sensory and affective responses.

Emotions take shape thanks to the colors, which we choose in absolute freedom to give voice to the sensations we are experiencing. Through a symbolic dimension, colors speak to us of the unconscious.

Concentration in the realization of a Mandala silences the exhausting dialogue of inner doubts, calms anxiety and daily tensions, and brings back harmony, naturalness, and the heart's rhythm, too often lost in the general din. Restlessness, dissatisfaction, anguish, loneliness, desire, or lack manifest as symptoms of the soul's discomfort that asks to be heard. Meditation is a tool to relax the mind and, consequently, the body, allowing our body to function better, heal better, and improve its performance through the energy that flows more fluidly.

The Sanskrit word Mandala means center or magic circle. It is a symbolic image in which two fundamental geometric shapes coexist: the square, which indicates the harmony to be achieved in the material world, and the circle, which is the consequent spiritual perfection.

The Mandala is an archetype that comes from the human soul and has always existed; it appears in every culture at different times and represents the model of life, and this is precisely the remarkable thing: the Mandala works beyond the knowledge and intelligence of various peoples, serves as an ancestral memory.

The space inside the ritual circle becomes a sacred space, and the only gesture of drawing the process is considered the act that puts in communication with the divine harmonies of the universe. It represents the continuity of life and the cyclical nature of existence. Drawing a Mandala invites you to a path that leads to discovering one's inner resources, abilities, and talent and exercises a rebalancing action between body and mind, which leads to a personal approach to strengthening individual resources and unexpressed potential.

In Hinduism and Buddhism drawing a Mandala represents the universe, its origins, and the relationships between the forces of the cosmos and the divine and is therefore considered a contemplative practice that allows you to grow internally.

The famous Swiss psychoanalyst Carl Gustav Jung, who has studied the subject for over twenty years, affirms that "Mandalas are one of the best examples of the universal operation of an archetype," that is, of the action of those dominant themes and patterns in the life of the man, which we can find in every culture, imprints present in the psyche as a mark of belonging to a race. According to Jung, during periods of psychic tension, mandalic figures can spontaneously appear in dreams to bring or indicate the possibility of inner order and to give expression and form to something that does not yet exist, to something new and unique.

Mandalas favor an inner recollection, help us find ourselves in the "here and now" of the experience, and find a balance in a particular moment or passage of our life. The Mandala is an image of ourselves that, through its realization, can increase our degree of consciousness and awareness. The incomplete aspects of identity are recomposed during its completion favoring the individuation process of "broadening the sphere of consciousness." While constructing the Mandala, man concentrates, individualizes himself, and carries out an interior search indispensable for catharsis and purification.

This is why, in particular with subjects with dissociative disorders, the constant use of Mandalas as a support to the psychotherapeutic path has a perfect effect. Mandala coloring has also been shown to be beneficial in relieving anxiety states. In general, it has proved to be particularly useful in treating certain forms of neurosis and psychosis in the psychotherapeutic field. In the medical field, the Mandala has been used therapeutically to treat cancer; in fact, it represents a way to rediscover order and energy, aspects that tend to be lost when one is sick. Workshops with Mandalas, proposed to disabled students to contain anxiety and stimulate their individuality and creativity, have favored processes of integration and self-expression. Coloring Mandalas is also a beneficial activity for children: the shapes and colors of the Mandala are an invitation to play and allow the child to concentrate, allowing him to achieve balance and tranquility.

**How to Make a Mandala**

A Mandala can be made using pre-existing drawings or freehand Mandalas. It can be made with fabrics, colors, sand, colored earth, powders, and elements present in nature. It can be drawn on paper or other media and kept or destroyed once finished and contemplated. The time to spend should be at least one hour in a calm and quiet environment. It can be helpful before starting to meditate for a while.

Freehand Mandalas can be made using compasses (not essential), pencil lines, paper, and colors. You decide whether to start from the center or the outside and let yourself be guided by your emotions and instincts until you feel that the Mandala is over. There are different approaches depending on the result you want to achieve.

The whole universe is an immense Mandala formed by innumerable other Mandalas: the eye is a Mandala, as well as the face, the hand, or the body; the moon and the sun are two magical mandalas.

Any form on which we can meditate or concentrate allows a period of detachment from the surrounding world and a greater concentration on ourselves.

Recommended for those suffering from anxiety: they relax the mind and promote the powers of clairvoyance and telepathy.

Mandalas are generally distinguished by the symbols, archetypes, moods they represent, and the therapeutic effects they reproduce.

Painting or coloring Mandalas helps us discover our stage of life and what mood we are in: everyone can express themselves through Mandalas.

Mandalas are used to create internal order, listen to the inner voice, focus on oneself, and express one's wholeness.

Mandalic forms strengthen the mind by awakening the energy points of the cerebral cortex and retracing the energy stored in our body. The Mandala is an excellent therapeutic path, a self-diagnosis, which can awaken dormant parts of the body and mind if you abandon yourself to the sensations and free associations implemented by the brain.

The Mandala highlights the various forms of consciousness and the path to enlightenment. It evokes a psychological course of inner exploration and cancels all mental dispersions that mislead the search for balance and centrality. Eliminating the fluctuations of thought focuses the attention on the desired point, "reprogramming" the brain autonomously.

The Saxon Mandala demonstrates how the Celtic tradition survived the Saxon conquest. In this brooch, Saxon motifs coexist with Celtic motifs. Below, the Mandala of the ancient Germans shows how the Germanic peoples (see representation in the Swedish sun wheel Gotland ) were spiritually united to the Mandala, found during the ancient warrior tribes of Scythians, Goths, Saxons, and others.

A more modern view of the Mandala is the computerized one: most of the technological world broadly refers to the Mandala, from the wheel's progress in its numerous aspects to the most recent product of the polarized world of contrasts it represents. Using the computer, it is also possible to imitate the ancient models of rosettes and stained-glass windows with surprising results and astonishing speed.

### The Colors: Blue

Blue is the color of the sky and water; it expresses receptivity, creativity, and spiritual power. Blue opens the door to imagination, dreams, and the unconscious. It is very relaxing and carries the qualities of decision, originality, and organizational spirit.

### The Colors: Yellow

Yellow is the color of the sun; it expresses joy, renewal, and communicativeness. It represents a highly developed intellect and an awareness of one's responsibilities. Gold represents contact with the divine, and black is the spectrum of the interaction of all colors.

### The Colors: Purple

Purple encourages self-awareness and reflects dignity, nobility, and self-esteem. It is the royal colour. Purple becomes the architect of human destiny on a psychic level, as its quality is in tune with vision and intuition. It is the colour associated with artistic abilities, tolerance, and consideration.

### The Colors: Orange

Orange is outgoing and decisive, like red, but more constructively. It reflects enthusiasm combined with a natural and intuitive liveliness. It brings self-confidence, strength and courage, and a positive attitude towards life.

### The Colors: Red

It is preferred by outgoing people to signify their openness, energy, and activity. Deep red expresses grounding and protection from earth energy, harmonizes the primary chakras, and fights energy deficiencies by restoring physical power. Helps all types of survival-related fear.

### The Colors: Turquoise

Turquoise encourages creative communication of the heart in all its shades and keeps the flow of enlightened communication connected to the sensitive part of being. It gives the necessary opening to express one's creativity, to express oneself directly from the heart, freeing oneself from fears and vulnerabilities. It encourages independence and the ability to take responsibility for one's feelings and actions.

### The Colors: Green

Green helps us find our space and get to the heart of things. Bring peace to the emotions through calm, rebalancing, and centrality. The heart chakra's color opens and calms; it helps to expand your

154

breathing.

**The Colors: Pink**

Pink represents the warmth and commitment to love ourselves and others; it envelops us in a cordial atmosphere that helps us to give our best. It brings emotional well-being by infusing love, care, and warmth.

www.ingramcontent.com/pod-product-compliance
Lightning Source LLC
Chambersburg PA
CBHW071151120626
46546CB00006B/2210